Developing Mathematical Ideas
Algebra

Patterns, Functions, and Change

Casebook

A collaborative project by the staff and
participants of Teaching to the Big Ideas

Principal Investigators
Deborah Schifter
Virginia Bastable
Susan Jo Russell

With
Stephen Monk
Tracy Noble

And teacher collaborators

DALE SEYMOUR PUBLICATIONS
Pearson Learning Group

National Science Foundation

Ex⤬onMobil

This work was supported by the National Science Foundation under Grant Nos. ESI-9254393 (awarded to EDC), ESI-9731064 (awarded to EDC), ESI-0095450 (awarded to TERC), and ESI-0242609 (awarded to EDC). Any opinions, findings, conclusions, or recommendations expressed here are those of the authors and do not necessarily reflect the views of the National Science Foundation.

Additional support was provided by a grant from the ExxonMobil Foundation.

Art & Design: Evelyn Bauer, Kamau DeSilva
Editorial: Jennifer Chintala, Margie Richmond, Jennifer Serra
Production/Manufacturing: Nathan Kinney
Marketing: Kimberly Doster

ISBN-13: 978-1-4284-0520-2
ISBN-10:   1-4284-0520-8

Printed in the United States of America
 3 4 5 6   V031 13 12 11 10

Dale
Seymour
Publications
Pearson Learning Group

1-800-321-3106
www.pearsonlearning.com

Teaching to the Big Ideas

The *Developing Mathematical Ideas* series was conceived by Teaching to the Big Ideas, an NSF Teacher Enhancement Project. *Patterns, Functions, and Change* was developed as a collaborative project by the staff and teacher collaborators of the Teaching to the Big Ideas and Investigations Revisions Projects.

PROJECT DIRECTORS   Deborah Schifter (Educational Development Center), Virginia Bastable (SummerMath for Teachers at Mount Holyoke College), and Susan Jo Russell (TERC)

CONSULTANTS   Stephen G. Monk (University of Washington), Tracy Noble (TERC), Virginia Stimpson (University of Washington), Christopher Fraley (Lake Washington School District), Thomas Carpenter (University of Wisconsin), Herbert Clemens (Ohio State University), Mark Driscoll (Education Development Center), Benjamin Ford (Sonoma State University), Megan Franke (UCLA), James Kaput (University of Massachusetts at Dartmouth), James Lewis (University of Nebraska), Jean Moon (National Academy of Sciences), Erna Yackel (Purdue University at Calamut)

TEACHER COLLABORATORS   Beth Alchek, Barbara Bernard, Nancy Buell, Rose Christiansen, Lisette Colon, Kim Cook, Fran Cooper, Pat DeAngelis, Pat Erikson, Marcia Estelle, Nikki Faria-Mitchell, Trish Farrington, Tom Fisher, Mike Flynn, Elaine Herzog, Kirsten Lee Howard, David Jesser, Liliana Klass, Melissa Lee, Jennifer Levitan, Kathe Millett, Florence Molyneaux, Elizabeth Monopoli, Robin Musser, Christine Norrman, Deborah Carey O'Brien, Mary Beth Cahill O'Connor, Anne Marie O'Reilly, Mark Paige, Margaret Riddle, Rebeka Eston Salemi, Karen Schweitzer, Lisa Seyferth, Susan Bush Smith, Shoshy Starr, Elizabeth Sweeney, Janice Szymaszek, Danielle Thorne, Karen Tobin, JoAnn Traushke, Ana Vaisenstein, Yvonne Watson-Murrell, Michelle Woods, and Mary Wright, representing the public schools of Amherst, Boston, Brookline, Holyoke, Lincoln, Natick, Newton, Northampton, South Hadley, Southampton, Springfield, Sudbury, West Springfield, Westwood, and Williamsburg, Massachusetts, and the Smith College Campus School in Northampton, Massachusetts

VIDEO DEVELOPMENT   David Smith (David Smith Productions)

FIELD-TEST SITES   Bismarck Public Schools (North Dakota), Boston Public Schools (Massachusetts), Buncombe County Public Schools (North Carolina), Eastern Washington University (Washington), Lake Washington School District (Washington), Northampton Public Schools (Massachusetts), Stafford County Schools (Virginia), Teachers Development Group (Oregon)

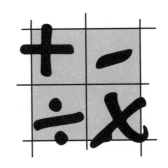

C O N T E N T S

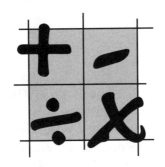

Introduction

A second-grade class was collecting lunch money; lunches each cost $2. Because one student had brought in a $20 bill to pay for future lunches, students began to offer ideas about how many lunches it would buy. Ezra thought it would pay for 10 lunches. Micah said that $10 would pay for 5 lunches. Jared asked how many lunches $5 would pay for. After a few moments of silence, Leah, who had been deep in thought, said, "Two and a half. You could get two-and-a-half lunches for $5." Then she giggled at the silliness of half a lunch.

Students in this class came upon a problem that involves two quantities—a number of dollars and a number of lunches—that vary in relation to each other. For any number of dollars, there is a certain number of lunches that it will buy: $2 pays for 1 lunch; $4 pays for 2 lunches; $6 pays for 3 lunches. This problem involving a correspondence from one set (number of dollars) to another (number of lunches) is an example of a *function*.

In this seminar, Patterns, Functions, and Change, you will explore a variety of examples of different kinds of functions: If you drop the same number of pennies into a jar each day, the number of pennies in the jar depends on the number of days you have been collecting pennies. If you are building squares out of square tiles, the number of tiles in your square depends on the number of tiles in one row. If you burn a candle, the height of the candle depends on the length of time it has been burning.

1

As you work with different kinds of functions, you will explore how such situations can be represented. You will consider conventional forms of representations—tables, graphs, and formulas written algebraically—as well as representations invented by students to keep track of a phenomenon that involves change. For example, how do second graders represent the money-lunch relationship? How does a change in the amount of money you have change the number of lunches you can buy?

You will explore a variety of features of a function and examine how these features appear in the different representations. Is the function increasing, decreasing, or staying the same? Is it increasing or decreasing at a steady rate, or is the rate of change varying?

The cases in the Casebook present students in elementary and middle school engaging with these and other ideas about functions. Like the other DMI module(s) you may have studied, the cases were written by elementary- and middle-school teachers recounting episodes from their classrooms. Most teachers had inclusive classrooms; a few worked in pullout programs exclusively with students with special needs. The range represents schools in urban, suburban, and rural communities. The teacher-authors, who were themselves working to understand the "big ideas" of the elementary- and middle-grade mathematics curriculum, wrote these cases as part of their process of inquiry. They came together on a regular basis to read and discuss each other's developing work.

The cases are grouped to present students in classrooms who are working on similar mathematical issues related to functions. Through the cases, you will examine students' early work with repeating patterns and explore how this work can be extended to support the study of functions; you will see students' early encounters with conventional and informal representations; and you will identify students' insights and confusions as they explore functional situations of greater complexity.

In the cases in Chapter 1, students work with repeating and growing patterns, a precursor to work with functions. Chapters 2 through 5 explore various aspects of linear functions: How are they represented? How can they be compared? What are the connections between linear relationships and direct proportions? Chapter 6 presents students' work with functions that can be defined by formulas but, when graphed, are not straight lines. In Chapter 7, the functions are not defined by formulas but instead by gathering data, such as the temperature outside the classroom at 9:00 a.m. on different days of the year.

Chapter 8, the last in the Casebook, is the essay "The Mathematics of Patterns, Functions, and Change for the K–8 Classroom." It reviews the ideas explored in the seminar, identifying recent research findings that touch on the issues explored in the cases (Chapters 1–7).

C H A P T E R

1

Using Patterns to Determine What's Ahead

In the elementary grades, students often work with different kinds of patterns: Some are repeating, patterns that have a fixed set of ordered elements (a unit) that repeats over and over. For example, in the pattern *a, b, c, a, b, c, a, b, c, …,* the unit that repeats is *a, b, c.* Students also work with number sequences determined by applying a rule to one number to get the next number. In the number sequence 1, 4, 7, 10, …, the number 3 is added to each element of the sequence to get the next element.

In this chapter, the cases are based on students in Kindergarten through Grade 4 exploring repeating patterns and number sequences in a variety of contexts. In all of the cases, students are learning about the power of patterns to determine what is ahead. In some of the cases, students go beyond the context of a particular pattern to explore common structures. For example, first graders in Case 3 consider two contexts that generate the same number sequence and see one as a representation of the other. In Case 4, fourth graders work with a repeating pattern to generate a number sequence.

Your reading of Cases 2, 3, and 4 will be enhanced if you first explore the mathematics activity the students are working on. The relevant activity is printed before each of these cases. Be prepared to give your work on these problems to your facilitator at the first session.

Patterns on the pocket chart

Catherine

KINDERGARTEN, FEBRUARY

Recently we have been learning to be "nature detectives" in preparation for an upcoming field trip to a science museum. The students have become very proficient at determining which animal might have left a certain track. I decided to combine our nature study with our study of patterns. I cut several two-inch squares to fit on our pocket chart and drew a variety of animal tracks on the cards. In the first row of the chart, I made an a, b, a, b pattern of paw marks from a cat and a dog; in the second row, an a, b, b, a, b, b pattern of prints from a deer and tracks from a bird; in the third row, an a, a, b, a, a, b pattern of footprints of a person and tracks from a bird. Each row had ten cards. I hid some cards in each pattern behind cards with a question mark.

Below is a diagram of what the pocket chart looked like when we started a whole-class discussion.

🐾	🐾	🐾	?	?	?	?	?	?	?
(deer)	(bird)	?	?	?	?	?	?	?	?
(feet)	(feet)	(bird)	?	?	?	?	?	?	?

TEACHER:	I want to see if you can be nature detectives. What do you see on the pocket chart?
MARTINA:	I see a dog and a cat.
ANIKA:	A deer.
SAVANNA:	A bird or duck.
TEACHER:	Look again. Can it be a duck?
SAVANNA:	No, a duck would have webbed feet. It is a bird.
MARTINA:	I followed some prints at my house and found that they had a line in the middle like that one (pointing to one of the bird cards).
TEACHER:	What was it?
MARTINA:	A bird.
LUCAS:	What are the question marks for?
CARLY:	We used them before.
KIM:	They're patterns. It's cat, dog, cat, dog.
TEACHER:	What do other people think?

15

20

25

LUCAS: It could be cat, cat, dog, dog.   30

KIM: No, it has to be cat, dog, cat, dog.

   I let Kim's comment go, even though with the information given,
students cannot know for sure which element comes next. The chart showed
the first three elements—cat, dog, cat—and so Lucas' idea could not be
correct. However, since I have not yet specified that it is an *a*, *b*, *a*, *b* pattern,   35
the next element could be anything. We will work on that issue when we get
to the next pattern, with tracks from a deer and a bird.

TEACHER: Any other ideas? (A long silence) Let's unveil this one.
           (By removing the first question mark, a dog paw is shown.)

KIM: See, it is a dog. Cat, dog, cat, dog.   40

TEACHER: Now, I'll tell you that the pattern continues: cat, dog, cat,
           dog. So, I want you to think about what goes here (pointing
           to the 8th card in the row).

RHEA: Cat.

MIKE: No, dog. (Lots of other children respond in unison.)   45

TEACHER: Raise your hand if you think it is a cat. (Rhea and two other
           children sitting near her raise their hands.) Raise your hand
           if you think it is a dog. (All other hands go up.) How do
           you know?

LUCAS: I counted cat, dog, cat, dog.   50

Catherine

TEACHER: What do you mean you counted?

LUCAS: Can I show you?

I nod yes, and Lucas comes up to the pocket chart.

LUCAS: See it goes cat, dog, cat, dog, cat, dog, cat, dog.

Lucas points to each card as he reads the pattern. He stops pointing   55
when his finger touches the 8th card.

TEACHER: I see how you touched each card as you read the pattern.
                Is this what you mean by counting?

LUCAS: Yes. It's like counting the numbers.

SHELLY: Or reading. We touch words.   60

MIKE: I started here and counted. (Mike moves up to the chart and
                places his finger on the fourth card, which is the last one
                exposed.) Dog, cat, dog, cat, dog.

KATHRYN: I started here. (Kathryn points to the 5th card.) I just knew
                it was a dog. See, cat, dog, cat, dog. (Kathryn touches cards   65
                6, 7, and 8, as she proceeds to the right across the row.)

TEACHER: Rhea, you've been waiting with your hand up for a long time.

RHEA: I changed my mind. I think it is a dog.

TEACHER: Why?

RHEA: I just know it is now. See…   70

Rhea approaches the chart and begins to read the pattern from the first
card like Lucas did.

RHEA: Cat, dog, cat, dog, cat, dog, cat, dog.

TEACHER: Let's see what happens when we take the question marks
                away.   75

Starting with the 5th card, I remove the question marks one at a time,
and the children respond with the name of the animal track that has been
concealed.

CLASS: (In unison) Cat, dog, cat, dog.

Catherine

🐾	🐾	🐾	🐾	🐾	🐾	🐾	🐾	?	?
🦌	🐦	?	?	?	?	?	?	?	?
👣	👣	🐦	?	?	?	?	?	?	?

When the 8th card was unveiled, there were lots of cheers.   80

CARLY: It had to be a dog.

TEACHER: Why?

CARLY: 'Cause that's how it works.

Carly's reply tells it the way most children see it. The repetition in this *a, b, a, b* pattern is simply "how it works." Though this phrase sums it up   85
in very unsophisticated terms, it tells a lot.

I believe a lot was said in this quick classroom exchange. The children were thinking seriously about the task at hand. In many ways, they were working alone during this discussion. Though they were thinking independently, they also listened to each other as a way to make sense of what   90
was going on. When Rhea commented that she had changed her mind, I believe she did so because other students had convinced her that her first idea was incorrect. It was exciting to see her think through her response and be willing to raise her hand to announce a change in her thinking.

At the same time, I am intrigued by the words Lucas used to describe   95
his strategy for making a prediction and at how Mike and Kathryn showed us glimpses of alternatives. Dialogue and discourse are now such a fundamental part of my classroom, and yet, I still wonder about what it takes for these young children to develop a strategy, solve the problem in their head, and then share their thinking with the class. It is a lot to expect of   100
five- and six-year-olds.

When I planned this activity, I posted three different patterns on the chart. Sometimes when we have worked on this activity, we have successfully worked through two or three different patterns. Today, the discussion

was richer, and thus we spent 15 minutes on the first row. Once the ten
cards were all unveiled, I decided to stop the discussion and not pursue
the other two patterns at this time. I always try to use the children as a
barometer for how long this type of whole-group discussion can last. They
were very invested in the discussion, but I felt if I pushed for a second or
third pattern, it would be too much in one sitting. We will get back to the
other two rows at another time.

MATH ACTIVITY: The next case is based on a third-grade class working on an activity called Staircase Towers. Before you read the case, take
a few minutes to explore this activity.

Staircase Towers: In Staircase Towers, students build stacks of cubes that
look like staircases. Below is a staircase tower that is made by starting
with 1 cube and adding 2 cubes to each successive tower. The amount
you start with is the "start with" number, and the amount you add is
called the "step up" number. In the illustration, there are 4 towers, and
the 4th tower has 7 cubes. You could continue to add more towers, each
time adding the "step up" number to the number of cubes in the previous tower. Your job is to figure out how many cubes are in each tower. For
instance, for this staircase the 10th tower will have 19 cubes.

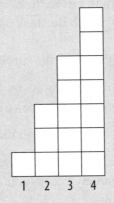

Now draw or build staircase towers using the following guidelines and
determine the number of cubes in the first 5 towers.

1. Start with 3. Step up 2 each time.
2. Start with 5. Step up 2 each time.
3. Start with 2. Step up 3 each time.
4. Start with 1. Step up 3 each time.

Catherine
KINDERGARTEN, FEBRUARY

Now that you have had a chance to work on this activity, read about a third-grade class working on the same activity. | 130

C A S E **2**

Staircase Towers

Lucy
GRADE 3, SEPTEMBER

Early in September, as I was getting to know the students in my class, I gave them a pattern activity to work on. I knew that the students had entered my class with a variety of experiences in the younger grades with repeating patterns. We were going to explore the growing patterns found | 135
in an activity called Staircase Towers. I recognized there would be many opportunities for counting and adding in the task, and I knew I could learn much about my students' thinking from the activity. I was not sure how each of the students would approach this task or what size numbers they could think about. | 140

I had prepared a worksheet on which the first problem read as follows:

> You will build several towers. The first tower has 1 cube. For each new tower, add 3 cubes more than the one you just made.
>
> After you have made a few towers, answer these questions:
>
> - What do you notice about your towers? What patterns do you see? | 145
> - Can you figure out how many cubes would be in the 10th tower? How do you know?

As soon as the class began working, I realized I had chosen a pattern that was difficult for some of the kids to think about because the numbers became large very quickly. However, it did give me much to consider about | 150
their understanding of patterns, number sense, counting, and addition.

Most of the children had no problem building the pattern. They got right to work and were marveling how fast the staircases were growing. There was much counting going on. Some children started over at 1 each time,

10

counting all the cubes in each new tower. Others were just counting on by 1s from the previous tower's total. Some students tried putting down only the 3 new cubes next to the top of the previous tower. They said this made it easy because they were just adding on 3 each time. A few of the children made the second tower with just 3 cubes but did add on 3 more each time. This caused their total to be off by 1 each time. Some students made counting errors and some made adding errors. So there were many conversations about what the correct amounts should be and much recounting and adding again.

Everyone built the towers out of cubes, realizing quickly the towers needed to be lying down because they were getting so tall so fast. Here are some of the ways the students wrote about the problem.

Stanley wrote on his paper in response to what he noticed: "They look like staircases. It gets taller." He drew the first 2 towers; then he wrote 7, 10, 13, 16, 19, 22, 25.

Burt wrote: "It keeps getting bigger. There are 3 more each time." In response to predicting how many would be in the 10th tower he began writing number sentences, "22 + 3 = 25, 25 + 3 = 28," and concluded there are 28 cubes in the 10th tower.

Jeff and Barry listed all the numbers for the first 10 towers because they built all 10 towers rather than make a prediction. So I asked them how many cubes would be in the 20th tower. Barry said it would be 10 more numbers. They both quickly started writing down the next 10 numbers in their pattern, 31, 34, 37, 40, 43, 46, 49, 52, 55, 58. They said it had to be 58 because there were 10 more numbers in their list and that was the 10 more towers to get to the 20th tower.

In the whole-group discussion at the end of class, we built the towers together, talking about students' thinking as we created the towers. We built several towers, and the class explained we needed 3 more cubes each time, that we could just count 3 from the previous tower to know how many would be in the next tower. We talked about their counting and adding strategies. When we had 8 towers, I asked how many cubes would be in the 10th tower.

ALLEN: Add on 6 more cubes and count them.

TEACHER: How come 6 more cubes?

ALLEN: Because that would make 10 towers.

TEACHER: I thought we had to add 3 cubes each time, and he's telling us to add 6!

ALLEN: Yeah, for 2 more towers. (Many kids were agreeing that it would be 6 more.) 3 + 3 is 6. It's 3 for each tower. 3 for one tower, and 3 more for the 10th tower.

I am not sure where the students are with their thinking about this type of growing pattern, but they were able to notice how changes were happening within the context of the patterns in these problems. Now I am wondering about what they will be able to do when they explore the ideas of changes over time later in the year.

195

MATH ACTIVITY: The next case is based on a first-grade class working on two different math activities: Staircase Towers and Penny Jar. You have already learned about Staircase Towers. Before you read the case, take a few minutes to explore Penny Jar.

200

Penny Jar: Imagine you have a jar in which to save pennies. You decide to save the same number of pennies each day. Before you start, the jar might already have some pennies in it. We call these the pennies you "start with." Given a certain number to start with and a certain number to add each day, your job is to see how many pennies you will have after 1, 2, 3, 4, … days. For example, perhaps there are 4 pennies in the jar to start with and you add 3 pennies each day. After you add one day's worth of pennies (Day 1), you have 7 pennies; then on Day 2 you add another 3, giving you a total of 10 pennies; on Day 3 you will have 13 pennies. Try some Penny Jar problems.

205

210

For the following situations, find the number of pennies in the jar for Days 1, 2, 3, …, up to 10.

215

1. Start with 3. Add 2 each day.
2. Start with 5. Add 2 each day.
3. Start with 2. Add 3 each day.
4. Start with 1. Add 3 each day.

Staircase Towers and Penny Jar

Gretchen

My first graders were comparing a Staircase Tower problem to a Penny Jar problem. In each case, the "start with" number was 1, and the number added repeatedly was 3. For some children, there was no discernible connection between the activities. They did not seem to notice that the numbers were the same until a peer pointed it out during the discussion. Others had the most nascent connections. "They both start at one," was as far as Eli could go.

However, some children could see similarities between the Staircase Towers and the Penny Jar. Out of the blue Anna said, "The Staircase Towers is really a graph of the Penny Jar." I asked her to say more. She explained that each square on the staircase tower was a penny. Each column showed how many you have in the penny jar that day. Benjamin added to what Anna was saying by pointing out that the numbers underneath the columns in the Staircase Towers matched the numbers of the Penny Jar, except for the starting number, which was 1. The 1 was the "start with" number in the Staircase Tower and it was the penny in the jar at the start for our Penny Jar pattern.

I was so intrigued that Anna saw the staircase tower as a graphic representation of the penny jar that I approached her later in the day to interview her further. When I asked how she figured out that the staircase towers were a graph of the penny jar, she said she could just "see it." She referred to our graphing board in the class.

When students arrive each day, they "sign in" on the graphing board by responding to a question that a class member has written. Each student has a cube labeled with his or her name. As they enter the classroom, students place their cube on the board to indicate their response to the question. By observing who has answered the question, I am able to determine who is present in class on that particular day. Sometimes the question is as basic as, "Did you brush your teeth this morning?" with yes and no as the choices.

220

225

230

235

240

245

Other questions are more complex, such as "Which Lego card did you think was the hardest to build?" The Lego card numbers are listed along the bottom of the graph and students place their cubes above the card number that they found most difficult to build. Most days begin with the class looking at the resulting bar graph and interpreting it in some way. With the Lego question it became clear that one particular card was considered harder than any other.

Looking at these graphs every day, Anna has developed a clear schema of a bar graph. While I never stopped to think that Staircase Towers could represent a bar graph for Penny Jar patterns, she recognized it immediately. To see the depth of her understanding, I showed her more Penny Jar problems and asked her if she could tell me what the Staircase Tower graph would look like for a few of them. She had no problem pointing to what was in the Penny Jar and describing it as the "start with" number for the Staircase Tower. She knew that what you added to the Penny Jar each day was the "step up" number on the graph. I found this very interesting because one of the aspects children struggled with while building Staircase Towers was how much to step up. The concept of adding more pennies to a jar each day seemed far easier for them to imagine and represent with a drawing.

The question that I am left with is, Can I do more to help other students see the connection Anna has made and how important is having this understanding in first grade?

MATH ACTIVITY: In the next case, a fourth-grade class is working with a repeating pattern to generate a number sequence. Before you read the case, take a few minutes to explore this activity, which is presented on lines 276–285.

Four-element repeating patterns

Lenora

GRADE 4 ESL, DECEMBER

My students were given an activity sheet involving patterns of colored cubes. They were shown a picture of a "cube train" and were told that the color pattern repeats. The number below each square identifies its position in the train. The cubes were colored red, blue, yellow, and green. | 275

R	B	Y	G	R	B	Y	G	R	B
1	2	3	4	5	6	7	8	9	10

The activity sheet listed the following questions:

> What is the pattern? | 280
> What is the color of the 16th cube?
> What numbers are all the blue cubes? What do you notice about all of these numbers?
> What numbers are all the yellow cubes? What do you notice about all of these numbers? | 285

When we came together to discuss their work on the sheet, Daisy started us off by identifying the pattern.

DAISY: Red, blue, yellow, and green are repeating.

JASON: They are in the pattern because they keep going on and on, without changing. | 290

The class unanimously echoed Daisy's and Jason's answers.
Here are their responses to the second question about the 16th cube:

DORA: Green.

TEACHER: How do you know that?

| DORA: | I put four blocks and then counted, R is 1, B is 2, Y is 3, G is 4, R is 5, B is 6, Y is 7, until I got to G is 16. | 295 |

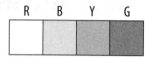

| TEACHER: | Why did you only count those four blocks? | |

| DORA: | Because that is the set that repeats. I don't need to make a giant line of cubes. I just keep counting the same four blocks, in the same order. | 300 |

| TEACHER: | Does anyone else have another way of figuring out what color the 16th cube will be? | |

| JUANITA: | I copied your pattern and then used it again. | |

| TEACHER: | Can you show me? | |

Juanita came to the board and drew the following: 305

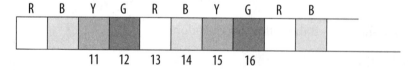

| TEACHER: | What about the first red and blue ones? | |

| JUANITA: | Because at the end of the line the red and blue had already been started. | |

Here are their responses to the third question about the blue cubes:

| CECILIA: | Blue is 2, 6, 10, 14, 18, 22 … It is counting by 4s. | 310 |

| JUANITA: | Some multiples of 2, if you skip. | |

| TEACHER: | Can you show me what you mean? | |

| JUANITA: | 2, 4, 6, 8, 10, 12, 14, 16, 18 … See the blue is every other multiple of 2. | |

| TEACHER: | Why are the blue ones not all multiples of 2? | 315 |

| MARCOS: | Because blue starts at number 2, but we are counting with a pattern of 4 cubes. Green gives the other multiples of 2 because it is the 4th cube. | |

Here are their responses to the fourth question about the yellow cubes:

TESSA: Yellow is 3, 7, 11, 15, 19… It is jumping by 4s just like the blue ones.

TEACHER: If it is jumping by 4s just like the blue ones, then why are they not landing on the same numbers?

BABETTE: Because they are starting at different numbers and then jumping 4 to the next color that is the same. Red is 1 + 4, blue is 2 + 4, yellow is 3 + 4, green is 4 + 4.

TEACHER: Why do we keep jumping by 4s?

BABETTE: Because there are only 4 colors repeating. If we had 6 colors repeating, it would be jumping by 6.

TEACHER: All of them?

CLASS: Yes.

On this pattern, the students started to delve further into making a formula for the given color by considering statements like "Red is 1 + 4." They recognized that even though there were 4 different colored cubes, each color was an equal distance to the next like color.

They went on to make a generalization that the number of jumps to get to a particular location would be dependent on the number of cubes in the repeating set. I was happy to see them use their ideas about multiples. I am eager to learn if they can continue to develop their ideas.

2

Representing Situations with Tables, Diagrams, and Graphs

CASE 5	Making sense of tables	Miranda	Grade 2, February
CASE 6	Lunch money models	Kate	Grades 1 and 2, September
CASE 7	Penny Jar arrays	Abigail	Grade 4, May
CASE 8	Graphing staircase problems	Lucy	Grade 3, January
CASE 9	Making sense of coordinate graphs	Karl	Grade 7, October

In each of the cases of this chapter, students are working with a *function*. The mathematical idea of "function" involves a correspondence from one set to another: Every item from the first set corresponds to exactly one item from the second. For example, in Case 5, second graders create "buildings" in which each floor has 3 rooms. The function is the correspondence from the number of floors in a building to the total number of rooms in the building. In Case 6, "Lunch money models," first and second graders explore the correspondence from the number of dollars they might have to the number of lunches they could buy. In Case 9, the class considers several different functions: The height of a tree in feet may be a function of how old it is; the temperature at a given location is a function of time.

Case 7 about the Penny Jar demonstrates that number sequences, like those explored in the previous chapter, can also be viewed as functions. The number of pennies in the jar corresponds to the number of rounds of adding pennies. In Case 8, the number of steps in a staircase tower corresponds to the position of the tower.

Students and teachers in these cases create a variety of representations of these functions and use their representations to explore the mathematical relationships more deeply. They make tables, create physical models, draw pictures, and produce graphs.

As you read the cases, consider how the representations used in one case might apply to another case. What would a table look like for the Penny Jar? How would you graph the floors-to-rooms relationship for the buildings or the money-to-lunch function?

C A S E   5

Making sense of tables

Miranda

GRADE 2, FEBRUARY

I recently introduced my second graders to tables with the goal of having them use tables as a representation to show how one variable changes in relation to another variable. For example, students were constructing buildings from cubes with the same number of "rooms" on each "floor." The number of floors could be represented by one variable and the total number of rooms in the building could be represented by a second variable. If the building has 3 rooms on each floor, for every increase of 1 floor, the total number of rooms in the building increases by 3. In this context they use a table to record the total number of rooms in relation to the total number of floors. They figure out the total number of rooms for successive floors up to 5 floors and then skip to 10 floors. Discussions are intended to focus on their strategies for figuring out the total number of rooms and

Miranda

GRADE 2, FEBRUARY

emphasize the meaning of individual rows of a table so that students are focusing on the relationship between the two variables.

At the end of our first day working on these activities, I sensed that my students were struggling to keep track of everything they were being asked to think about. For many of them, just constructing the buildings and figuring out the increasing number of rooms was a challenge. They did not seem to see the table as a tool for keeping track of how the building grew, much less to think about the number relationships within the table. They were working so hard to create the table that they did not step back and reflect on the information the table held. I began thinking about what I could have done differently and what I could do next to help them recognize that tables could be a useful tool.

Coincidentally, something happened in my classroom in connection with our calendar that related to this topic. We build our monthly calendar from a set of individual cards that create visual patterns. This month's calendar alternates pictures of snowmen, hats, and mittens. In years past, I have spent time focusing on these patterns with my students. Time constraints have pushed those discussions aside this year, and I have been waiting for the students to notice some of the patterns on their own. Last week, I noticed a small group of students looking at the calendar and discussing the pattern. Our calendar was complete to the 10th day.

The following morning I decided to use interest in the pattern on the calendar as an opportunity to look at tables in a different context. The 11th piece had been added and I asked the class to talk about what they noticed.

1	2	3	4	5	6	7
8	9	10	11			

Several students commented on the basic repetition of snowman, hat, and mittens. I drew their attention to the dates that were associated with the pictures. I asked on which day of the month the 1st hat appeared, the 2nd hat, and so on up to the 4th hat on the 11th day. Then I asked them on what number the 5th hat would appear. Several hands shot up. Everyone agreed that it would occur on the 14th because we added on 3 days each time. Then I asked about the 6th hat. Fewer hands went up. It seemed to be more difficult for them to keep track with nothing more than the blank spaces in front of them.

I drew a quick table and asked the students to help me fill in what we had noticed so far on the calendar:

Number of Hat	Number of Date
1	2
2	5
3	8
4	11

Once again, I asked about the 5th hat. We filled in 14. Then I skipped the 6th hat and asked for the 7th hat. The initial reaction was puzzled looks; then some hands shot up. Lindsay said the number would be 20. When I asked her how she got her answer, she demonstrated that she used her fingers to keep track of the hat number while counting on 3 each time. Next I asked for the 10th hat. Several hands went up again. From here we filled in the table for the days we had skipped. We stopped at the 10th hat because beyond that we would go past the number of days in the month.

By the end of this discussion, the majority of my students appeared engaged and seemed to understand what was going on. While we were not looking at number relationships between variables and were instead focusing on the counting pattern in one column, my students were reading across rows and seemed to have more control over the tool, at least this one aspect. A table helps you to keep track, so if you cannot use it for this very basic purpose, how will you use it as a tool for reflection?

Later on, as my students returned to their work with buildings of cubes, I circulated around the room, checking to see if students were making connections between their buildings and their tables. They were all able to show what each number on the table represented in their buildings. Many of them were noticing patterns in the rows and the columns. Several were doubling the number of rooms in 5 floors to find the number of rooms in 10 floors. While some of their increased comfort may have been a result of the previous day's struggle, my sense was that there was some carryover from the calendar discussion.

Next year, I will have my second graders spend more time trying to come up with their own ways of keeping track of how their buildings grow before introducing "my way." We will spend more time engaged in this keeping-track aspect of using tables before we go mining for the golden ideas that are found inside.

C A S E **6**

Lunch money models

Kate

Three days into the current school year, my first- and second-grade students spontaneously began to talk about something that surprised me.

I was doing the lunch count. Conveniently, lunches in our school cost $2. On Friday, Ezra brought in a $20 bill to pay for future lunches, and the children began to offer ideas about it. Ezra said that he thought that for the $20 he would be able to buy 10 lunches. Galen agreed. I asked how they knew, and another child offered that each lunch cost $2, so 10 lunches would cost $20. Someone else added that for $10 you could get 5 lunches. Jared asked how many lunches you could get for $5. I knew we had only moments before we had to leave the room for art class, so I quickly tried to record some of what they were saying on chart paper so we would not lose it. After a few moments of silence, Leah, who had been deep in thought, said, "Two and a half. You could get two-and-a-half lunches for $5." Then she giggled at the silliness of half a lunch.

As often happens, there was no time to finish this interesting conversation when it arose. We had to go to art class and would need to return to this discussion later.

We did not return to the discussion for about two weeks. I was trying to figure out how and when to reintroduce it to the class so that I could recapture their enthusiasm. I also wanted to be sure that there was an entry point for all of my first and second graders. I knew that most of my first graders were counting by 1s and would not yet be able to think about those chunks of 2 in a meaningful way. There had to be a way to help make this activity accessible to them and at the same time engaging to the second graders in the class who could not only count by 2s but had also expressed in that initial conversation some understanding of the relationship between the number of dollars and the number of lunches.

Initially, I made two decisions regarding the discussion. One decision was that we would explore this during a time other than our math period so that it would have a different feel for the children. The other decision was that I would reintroduce the scenario by having students show what they already understood about the problem. I mulled over in my head how they could do that, and I kept coming back to the same issues. It was still quite early in the year, and I wanted to make this an activity in which everyone could be successful. That meant not asking my first and second graders to write what they understood, nor to have a lengthy conversation. So, where would I start? It finally came to me that the place to start was with models. Students would use a representation, such as cubes or pictures, to demonstrate what they understood.

It has become clear to me over the past few years that when children use models to show what they understand, it serves several purposes. First, and for me foremost, is that it enables more children to express their understanding, and it gives more children a way to follow what others are saying. Because there are a variety of models that correspond to various learning styles, children can find the way to express themselves that fits best with how they learn. They also have representations other than spoken words to help them make sense of another person's thinking.

Having different models can also help us to "unpack" the mathematics that is being explored. By comparing two models and thinking about their similarities and differences, we can sometimes look more deeply at the underlying mathematics.

So last Wednesday I reintroduced the context. "The other day, Ezra brought in some lunch money, and he said, 'I know if I have this much money, I can get these many lunches.' All sorts of people started shouting out, 'Oh, I know if I had this much I could get ...' and so I started thinking about that whole idea of how much each lunch costs and how many lunches you would get if you had a certain amount of money. So my first question is what one lunch costs." The class answered me, "$2."

I asked Moira if she could show me with cubes how much one lunch costs. She put 2 cubes together and held that up. I then asked the others how Moira was showing the $2. I wanted to make sure that the children understood how the cubes were being used.

Abigail said that Moira was showing us the $2 that she could use to buy 1 lunch. When I probed further, she said that Moira put 2 cubes together. Leah's hand shot up and she added, "Each cube represents a dollar." What a great way to phrase it! I was so pleased to hear this coming from one of my second graders. This is one of the benefits of having students for two years. We talked about that for a minute because I wanted to reinforce the idea of the cube representing something else. I asked if I could use the cube to pay for the lunch (or for anything else). Of course they all said no. Sometimes my students think I am so silly when I ask questions like that, but I wanted to make the point.

Next I asked, if 1 lunch costs $2, then what would 2 lunches cost? I alerted the class to the fact that I had made a table to record the answers. Kayla said, "If 1 lunch costs $2 and 2 plus 2 is 4, then it must be that it's $4."

Number of Lunches	Number of Dollars
1 lunch	2 dollars
2 lunches	4 dollars
3 lunches	
4 lunches	
5 lunches	

At this time, I introduced the rest of the activity. "I would like you to use the cubes to show me how much 1 lunch costs, 2 lunches cost, 3 lunches, 4 lunches, 5 lunches, all the way up to 10 lunches. I'd like you to, using Leah's word, represent how much the lunches would cost all the way up

to 10 lunches using cubes." I made sure they all understood the task, and
then I handed out cubes to pairs of children.

    The children began their work quite enthusiastically. I was glad to see
them getting right to work because I still was not sure that all the children
were going to be engaged in the activity. As I began to see their models
emerge, I was surprised at how many different models there were. I had
expected to see many pairs making staircases that looked like this:

    I had pictured each fact being shown separately: 1 lunch, 2 cubes;
2 lunches, 4 cubes. I actually only saw one pair of students, Abigail and
Kayla, with a representation that looked like that.

    I was surprised to see that Pedro and Galen had one long train of 20
cubes. When I asked how to see the cost of any number of lunches, Pedro
pointed to the first 2 cubes and said that it was 1 lunch and $2. Then he
pointed to those 2 and the next 2 and said that it was 2 lunches and $4.
They had them all embedded into one train!

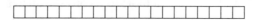

    Moira and Justin made groups of 2 and then put the groups together.
I heard Justin say, "You're always adding 2 more."

    Eliana and Anna worked next to each other, but each ended up making
her own model. Eliana made a pyramid of groups of 2. It looked like this:

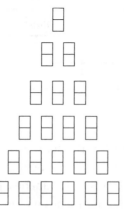

160

165

170

175

Interestingly, when we finally shared the models, Eliana had lost track of what in her model represented a lunch and what represented a dollar. I thought this was interesting because her construction looked so clear, but she had to think it through again to figure it out.

Anna's model had two trains for each relationship she was representing. For 1 lunch, she had a train of 1 cube and a train of 2 cubes. The first train represented the number of lunches, and the other, the number of dollars. I wonder if she was struggling with the same confusion as Eliana. When you have just one train (2 cubes), where is the lunch and where is the dollar? Anna avoided that problem by marking the dollars and the lunches separately.

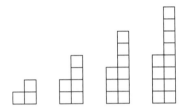

By the time we did our sharing on Friday, Micah and Thom, and Ezra all had representations that were like Anna's. In describing his and Thom's representation, Micah said that he always knew how many dollars for any number of lunches. He held each of a pair of trains in one hand and explained, "This (gesturing with the number-of-lunches train in his left hand) plus this (again gesturing with the same train) equals this" (referring to the longer train in his right hand that represented the number of dollars). "Wow," I said, "Does that always work?" "I think so," he replied.

Charlotte worked with Ezra but had a different model. She showed me a train of 10 cubes and said that she knew it was $20. She said that she counted each one, 1, 2, 3, ... 10. Then she counted them again, starting at 11. When I asked her why she counted them again, she said, "I counted them again because each lunch was $2."

Jared slowly got around to putting cubes into pairs, and with some support, figured out what to do with them. Margot, his partner, was carefully making trains of 2.

Leah and Finn began by making trains of 2, each train to represent a lunch. They originally had them grouped so that there was a single train (1 lunch); then they added one train to show a group of 2 lunches; then added another train for a group of 3 lunches, and so on. By the end of their action, it looked like this:

As they kept working and making more trains of 2, it all became one group. When they shared their representation, Leah said, "Here is 1 lunch, here's another lunch ..." It had almost the same feel as Pedro and Galen's. The 1 lunch did not need to be separate from the 2 lunches; the 1 was embedded in the 2.

I wonder now if I really can assume something about the children's understanding based on the model they chose to construct.

C A S E   7

Penny Jar arrays

Abigail

GRADE 4, MAY

We started working with penny jars three days ago. In this activity, students figure out how many pennies are in the jar if you start with a certain number and add a fixed number of pennies each round. For example, a Penny Jar card might read: 7 pennies to start; add 4 pennies each round. Students are asked to find and record how many pennies would be in the jar after Rounds 1 through 7 and also after Rounds 10, 15, and 20. The ideas were new to the class; everyone had access to the problems, and everyone was engaged.

From the beginning, there were differences in how students approached the problems. Some students used chips to represent the problem, counting on as they added each successive round of chips. Others did not use chips but instead added 4 to their previous total to find the next total. To find the total number of pennies in Round 10, some students first found the number of pennies in Rounds 8 and 9. Others saw that the three rounds from 7 to 10 would require 12 more pennies (3 rounds, 4 pennies per round) and added the 12 without finding the total for Rounds 8 and 9.

A few students were multiplying the number of the round by 4 to get the number of pennies that would be put in the jar and then added the pennies that were there at the start. This was an idea I wanted everyone to think about, so I gave it some prominence during our class discussion. I noticed more and more students using this multiplication technique as we continued to work with the penny jar over the next couple of days.

I was concerned about a number of students. I had expected students to be able to see how to go from Round 7 to 10 without having to calculate the intervening steps, but some were stuck on adding on each round and had no strategy for skipping rounds. Others were trying to follow the multiplication strategies they saw during discussion, but they could not explain how the strategy related to the situation. That is, they might write $(4 \times 10) + 7$, but they could not explain what the 4×10 represented or why it worked. The lack of connection to the situation showed up in their errors as well. When someone wrote $(7 \times 10) + 4$, these students had trouble figuring out which of the two number sentences represented "7 pennies to start; add 4 pennies each round."

I decided to return to the pennies and the jar with a small group of students and help them to visualize what was happening and how it related to the number sentences. I also hoped that the work with visualizing would move some students from thinking about the problem additively to thinking multiplicatively. Although the situation uses the term *add*, students need to multiply in order to figure out how many pennies are in the jar without counting every round. This is a huge shift for some fourth graders. I felt the image of dropping pennies into a jar only reinforced the idea of adding on. So, I used a different model this time; one in which they could see all of the pennies, but the added pennies were arranged in an array.

I drew a paper penny jar and had chips to represent pennies.

Omar picked a Penny Jar situation card: 4 pennies to start; add 3 pennies each round. We put the "start" pennies on the bottom of the paper penny jar, and I drew a line above them. Then students took turns adding the next rounds, lining them up neatly in rows. After each round, I drew a line above the pennies. When the jar was partly full, I asked how many rounds we had and how many pennies were in the jar.

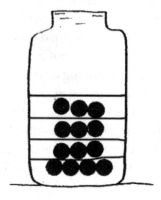

TEACHER: How many rounds do we have?

ERIN: 4, no 3. You don't count the start pennies.

TEACHER: How many pennies are in the jar?

STEPHANIE: 13. 4 + 3 = 7; 7 + 3 = 10; 10 + 3 = 13. I started with the start number and just added 3s.

TEACHER: Did anyone solve it a different way?

CATHY: 3 × 3 = 9. And we started with 4 pennies, so plus 4 equals 13 (9 + 4 = 13).

TEACHER: Show us the 3 × 3 in the jar.

Cathy pointed to the 3 rows of 3 pennies. We continued filling the jar.

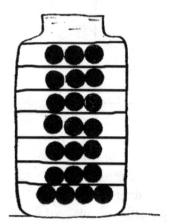

TEACHER:	How many pennies do we have now?	
KARL:	22. We have 6 rounds of 3; 3, 6, 9, 12, 15, 18, and then 4 more is 22.	275
TEACHER:	How many have we put in the jar, not counting what we started with?	
FREDDY:	18	
TEACHER:	How many did we start with?	
STEPHANIE:	4	280
TEACHER:	How many are in the jar?	
STEPHANIE:	22	

We worked through several situations together, talking about where we could see the start pennies and where the added pennies were represented. We also talked about how to find out how many ⟨285⟩ pennies were added. Some found the array model useful in knowing what to multiply. Others continued to think about the situation as 3 + 3 + 3 ... I would then ask, "Is there another way to write that?" One of my goals was to have students see these two parts of the situation, the start pennies and the added pennies. Also, I hoped that the array ⟨290⟩ formed by the pennies in the jar would move them to use multiplication in solving the problem.

As students returned to work independently or with a partner, some carried these ideas into their work. Because we have been using arrays to think about multiplication in other contexts, some students could now use ⟨295⟩ the image of the array to think about how multiplication applies to the penny jar. Others reverted to adding each round. They will need to explore these relationships further. Of course, some students are not very confident about their multiplication skills. They try to use repeated addition for most multiplication problems in other contexts, too. ⟨300⟩

I am left with questions about how visuals can help students organize the information to develop a strategy without simply giving them a picture to count. Can a concrete model help students think more abstractly?

Graphing staircase problems

Lucy

Early in the school year, my class had explored Staircase Towers. Later, they revisited the activity and recorded the number of cubes in each tower for several different growing patterns. They produced the following tables:

Table A1: start with 1, step up 1

Step Number	Number of cubes
1	1
2	2
3	3
4	4
5	5
6	6
7	7

Table A2: start with 1, step up 2

Step Number	Number of cubes
1	1
2	3
3	5
4	7
5	9
6	11
7	13

Table A3: start with 1, step up 3

Step Number	Number of cubes
1	1
2	4
3	7
4	10
5	13
6	16
7	19

Table B1: start with 2, step up 1

Step Number	Number of cubes
1	2
2	3
3	4
4	5
5	6
6	7
7	8

Table B2: start with 2, step up 2

Step Number	Number of cubes
1	2
2	4
3	6
4	8
5	10
6	12
7	14

Table B3: start with 2, step up 3

Step Number	Number of cubes
1	2
2	5
3	8
4	11
5	14
6	17
7	20

Table C1: start with 3, step up 1

Step Number	Number of cubes
1	3
2	4
3	5
4	6
5	7
6	8
7	9

Table C2: start with 3, step up 2

Step Number	Number of cubes
1	3
2	5
3	7
4	9
5	11
6	13
7	15

Table C3: start with 3, step up 3

Step Number	Number of cubes
1	3
2	6
3	9
4	12
5	15
6	18
7	21

Lucy

The children were intrigued by the number relationships they found in some of the tables. It was clear to many why the number pattern was changing the way it was, that the total depended on where they started and what was added. | 310

Recently, I asked the class to try to graph the data in these tables of cube totals. The students had previously worked with different kinds of graphing activities: graphing categorical data and creating line plots to represent numerical data. Also, as a whole-class morning routine, we had been reading the outside temperature once a week and recording it on a large graph. | 315
The class had begun to look at how the graph showed increasing and decreasing temperatures. However, this had not given individual students an opportunity to work through how to create this type of graph. Now I was interested in how they would represent the Staircase Tower data, what | 320
they would see as important to pay attention to.

We started as a whole group. I hung some poster paper with grid lines and asked students to think about how to graph the data in the tables, starting with Table A1.

Adam came up and said we could use a line plot. Below the line, he | 325
wrote the numbers 1 through 9 and then put 6 Xs above the 2.

```
    X
    X
    X
    X
    X
    X
_____
1 2 3 4 5 6 7 8 9
```

I asked Adam what all the Xs were, and he replied, "How many numbers." As I was thinking about what to ask next to try to figure out his thinking, he reconsidered what he had drawn and said we would have to use "a graph like that," pointing to our temperature graph. | 330

Next Adam drew a horizontal line perpendicular to a vertical line. Then he wrote 1–7 on the horizontal line and decided they were the step numbers, and 1–7 on the vertical.

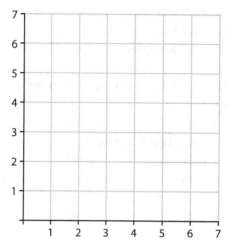

After Adam had drawn the two axes, I asked the class to look at what he had done so far and think about how we could put the data on his graph. "How would we show that in Step 1, there is 1 cube?" 335

Adam quickly put a dot at (1, 1).

TEACHER: Does anyone know what Adam is thinking? Can someone show us Step 2?

Ruben put a dot at (2, 2). 340

RUBEN: It's almost like the cube towers.

TEACHER: Whoa! It's like the cube towers?

STANLEY: Yeah, it's diagonal.

MIKIEL: It's going to go higher and higher.

TEACHER: Can someone put the third step on so we can see if it's 345
really true?

TaMara put the next dot at (3, 3). I asked how she knew where to put that dot, and she pointed to the 3 on the vertical axis and said it's 3 cubes. Then Abbi came up to put on the fourth step.

TEACHER: What's happening here? 350

MARIA: It's going up.

TEACHER: What kind of an up is it?

MARIA: A diagonal up.

We finished the last steps together. Now our graph looked like this.

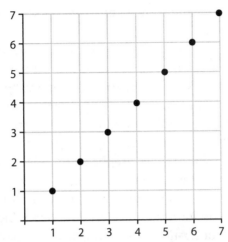

When we looked at the graph together, Jeff said we should connect the dots. I pointed out we could do that, to help us see the change, but only the dots are part of the graph. After all, we do not have a step number that is $2\frac{1}{2}$.

TEACHER: What kind of a line will it make?

MARIA: Straight.

ABBI: Diagonal.

RUBEN: It will make part of a triangle.

With the line drawn in, the graph now looked like this:

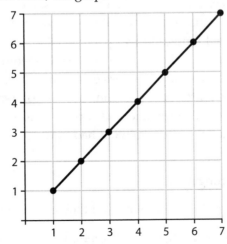

MARIA: You can see the stairs in the line.

Maria came up to the graph and showed the over-1-and-up-1 pattern for growth between each dot.

After this whole-class work, I sent my students off with the data tables and asked them to make graphs showing the data. I asked them what they thought their graphs would look like. Were they all going to be the same or different? How might they be different or the same? TaMara said they had to be different because there were different numbers in the tables. Maia commented that some of the numbers went much higher than others.

Most of the children were able to create graphs for the tables, but several questions came up. Where were they to start counting or labeling the graphs? Some kids put 1 at the intersection of the horizontal and vertical axes; some put the 1 on the horizontal axis one space over from the vertex, but one space up on the vertical axis they put 2. Another issue was whether they were to label lines or spaces, and whether points appear at intersections of the lines or not. A big question was about whether step numbers were on the vertical or horizontal axis. I did not clarify these issues at this time. We would look at the different graphs later and discuss the need for agreeing on conventions.

Adam asked me to help him because something was not coming out right. He told me his graph was "going over 3 and up 1" for each dot. I saw that he had labeled the horizontal axis as step numbers, but the points he plotted reversed the axes. I pointed at (4, 2) and asked him what it meant. He said it was 2 cubes at Step 4. I referred him to the table, and he quickly saw that he had meant to plot 4 cubes at Step 2.

Adam had another concern that he wanted to discuss. He was bothered that one of his dots was too close to the others; it was not following his over-3-and-up-1 pattern. I thought it was pretty cool that he noticed the pattern and could articulate it. I asked why it was happening, and he calmly replied, "It's because we added 3 cubes each time." I asked him to read the numbers along the bottom of his graph, and he realized he had skipped the number 15. "Oops," he smiled and corrected his graph.

At the end of class I asked the children what had made this work tricky. Among the responses were:

■ I put numbers in the wrong spots.

■ I didn't know where to put the numbers. Did they go up or down?

■ Which numbers to write and where to put them. What were the cubes and what were the steps?

I asked if it made a difference which axis we used for step numbers or number of cubes. Did the graphs look different? TaMara said it did not make a difference in the first graph because both steps and cubes had the same numbers (1–7). Then we compared two other graphs that represented the same data, but the axes were switched. On Jeff's graph, the number of cubes was on the *x*-axis, and Maia had put the step numbers on the *x*-axis.

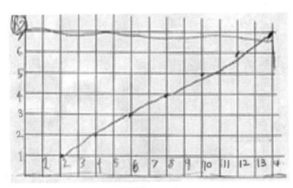

Jeff's graph of B2 (start with 2, step up 2)

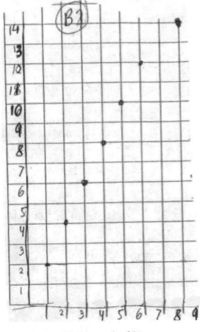

Maia's graph of B2

ELIZABETH: The lines go in the opposite direction.

MARIA: Maia's is going more up, and Jeff's is going more across.

BEN: Maia's is more slanted, and Jeff's is more flatter, less slanty.

I suggested we compare some graphs whose axes were oriented the same way. Ruben had a graph of Table C3, start with 3 and step up 3. I held it next to Maia's graph of B2.

410

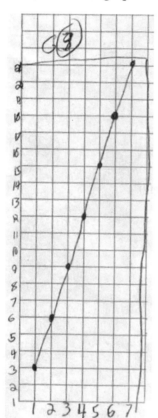

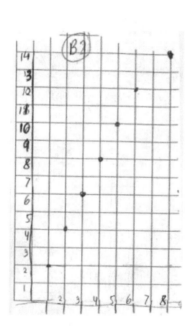

Ruben's graph of C3 (start with 3, step up 3)   Maia's graph of B2 (start with 2, step up 2)

Several kids said that Ruben's graph is "more up."

TEACHER: Why do you think Maia's graph is flatter? Or Ruben's is more up?

ELIZABETH: Because the numbers are higher. They are higher with the cubes. (She points to the vertical axis on Ruben's graph, which goes up to 21; Maia's goes up to 14.)

415

TEACHER: How many cubes did we add each time to Ruben's graph?

STUDENTS: 3

TEACHER: How many cubes did we add each time to Maia's graph?

STUDENTS: 2

I put Ruben's graph of C3 and Lynn's graph of B3 up for the children to examine.

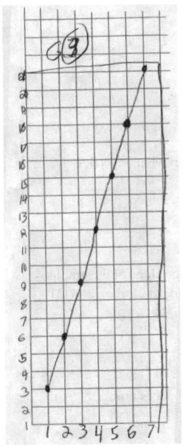 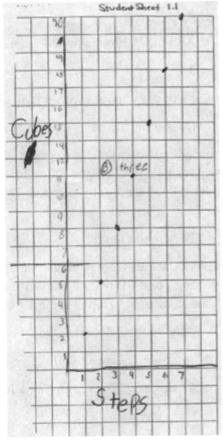

Ruben's graph of C3 (start with 3, step up 3) Lynn's graph of B3 (start with 2, step up 3)

MARIA: They look the same.

ALLEN: Yeah, they look the same.

YOSHI: It's B3 and C3.

JEFF: B3 and C3 look exactly the same.

As I took a closer look at the graphs, I saw that although Ruben and Lynn had both chosen the same variables for each of the axes, they had numbered the *y*-axis differently. If Ruben had made the point (0, 0) the intersection of the axes as Lynn had, all the points on his graph would have been shifted up one space. We would get back to that. For now, I wanted the class to see what aspect of the context gave the graphs the same slope.

TEACHER: Look at your data tables for B3 and C3. What is happening in B3? How many cubes are you adding each time?

MAIA: 3

TEACHER: And in C3, how many cubes are we adding each time?

MARIA: 3

ELIZABETH: I wonder what A3 would look like?

TEACHER: Does someone have a graph of A3?

[Note to reader: Create your own graph of A3. In what ways does it look the same as B3 and C3? How is it different?]

We put it next to the other two graphs. The kids chimed in that it looks like B3 and C3.

MARIA: They're the same.

At this point the kids were paying attention to the slope of the graphs, not their starting points. While A3 starts at 1 cube, B3 at 2 cubes, and C3 at 3 cubes, the slope of the graphs is the same.

TEACHER: Why do they all look alike?

ELIZABETH: Because they are all adding 3 cubes on.

TEACHER: All three of these graphs are adding 3 cubes on?

ADAM: Yeah, it works.

TaMARA: They have to be the same.

ELIZABETH: Yeah. They're all adding 3 on.

ABBI: They all look just like each other.

Making sense of coordinate graphs

Karl

GRADE 7, OCTOBER

As I was preparing to start a unit on graphing in my seventh-grade math classes, I was curious about what students already understood about coordinate graphs and the conventions of plotting points. I know that in their science class, students began the year with a unit that involved graphing data; so I was thinking that they would already be pretty comfortable with the process of setting up a coordinate system and plotting data on the graph. However, I also know that when students are initially trying to make sense of systems that involve the coordination of multiple features such as area (coordinating square units into length-and-width arrays) or bar graphs (coordinating the value of data with the frequency of that value), what seems obvious to us as adults can be very complex to someone still trying to sort out the relationships and conventions involved.

Since the beginning of the year, my math classes and I had been considering the power of representations to help us notice features, patterns, and relationships that might not be obvious otherwise. The representations that we had been working with to this point were diagrams, physical models, verbal descriptions, and contextual situations. Students were also coming to realize that representations are powerful tools to help us solve problems. The features, patterns, and relationships they were discovering were very useful in helping them to develop approaches to solve problems.

I used this previous work to introduce our next unit.

TEACHER: What is a variable? (I write the word on the board and give students a few moments to think.)

DAMON: It is where the numbers change.

YASH: It is like in a science experiment. There are things you can change.

Karl

TEACHER:	What things change?	485
YASH:	Maybe the temperature.	
MARY:	The height of something. Like a tree. (At this point, many hands go up as students begin to think of things that change.)	
TEACHER:	So Damon spoke of numbers changing, and many of you are telling me about objects or phenomena changing. Are we talking about the same thing?	490
DAMON:	I think so.	
JACOB:	Temperature changes numbers. (I see some heads nodding.) As the temperature goes up the numbers go up.	
MARY:	I was thinking numbers when I thought of how far a tree had grown. It might start out at 1 foot and then become 3 feet.	495
TEACHER:	These ideas connect well with the meaning of *variable* in mathematics. In math, a variable is a quantity that changes or an amount of something that changes. With the tree, the height changes as it grows older and we can use numbers to represent the amount of height it has. In math, just like in science, we often want to know how the change in one thing relates to the change in another. So, we might want to know how the amount of water given to a tree has an impact on the height of the tree. Both the amount of water and the height of the tree are variables that we can specify using numbers: perhaps number of feet for the height of the tree and number of gallons for the amount of water.	500 505

As we look at a situation involving several variables, it is often helpful to represent the variables using a table or a graph. Like diagrams and models, graphs are another way to represent something we are trying to make sense of. I know all of you have worked with bar graphs. How many of you have used coordinate graphs? (Most students raise their hands.) A coordinate graph is a nifty way to represent data from a situation to help us see how two variables might be related. Let's see what you already know about these kinds of graphs. I want you to take 2 minutes in your Think Teams to list everything you know about coordinate graphs.

510

515

Representing Situations with Tables, Diagrams, and Graphs

As I walk around and observe, I see that many Think Teams (groups of three) are drawing an example of a coordinate graph. Some of these look like big plus signs and others are in an *L* shape.

TEACHER: So what is a coordinate graph all about?

KRISTI: You make one by drawing a cross and putting little marks on the lines for where the numbers go.

TEACHER: Like this? (I draw a cross-hair figure and put tick marks on the lines, with some of the tick marks closer together than others.)

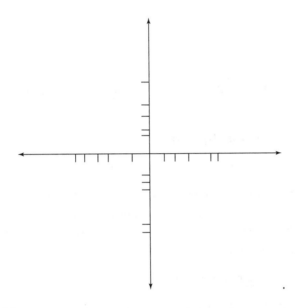

KRISTI: Yes.

MARK: But I don't think the tick marks are like that. They need to be the same distance apart.

I adjust the tick marks. I consider asking why they need to be the same distance apart, but I decide to wait because I know we will have many opportunities to discuss this in future lessons when they will have contexts to help clarify and refine their ideas.

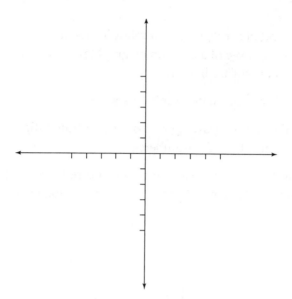

JACOB: Our group knows that the line that goes up is the *y* and the
            other is the *x*.

TEACHER: What do you mean by *y* and *x*?

JACOB: You put those letters at the ends of the lines.

TEACHER: (I put the letters at the end of the lines). Can anyone explain   540
            to me what the *y* and *x* are? (I am not sure what they under-
            stand about these labels. Everyone is quiet, and so I decide
            for now to move on.)

TEACHER: What else do you know about coordinate graphs?

YASH: Parts of it are positive and negative. You need to put   545
            numbers on the little lines so you can put dots on it.

KRISTI: Yeah, like 1, 2, 3, 4 starting with the marks to the right of
            where the lines cross. (I have Kristi come up to the board to
            put the numbers on, and she puts 1, 2, 3, 4, 5, 6, 7, and 8 on
            the right side of the horizontal line and the same numbers on   550
            the upper part of the vertical line.)

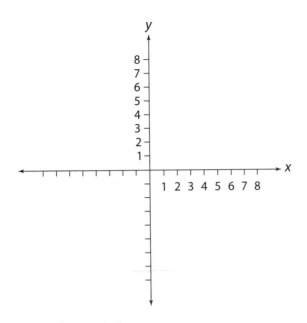

TEACHER: Yash talked about putting dots on the graph. How does that work? (A couple of hands go up. I call on James.)

JAMES: Can I come up and show you? (He comes to the board and writes the numbers 1 and 3.) You have to take two numbers and then use those to figure out where to put the dot.

555

TEACHER: Just a minute, James. In math, we call these two numbers a coordinate pair and we write them like this: [I write (1, 3) on the board]. OK, James, now what?

560

JAMES: The 1 is the *x*, so you start at the place where the lines cross, and you go up 1. The 3 is the *y*, so you go from the *y* line across 3. (James has reversed the way that you are supposed to plot points. A couple of hands shoot up.) Kristi?

565

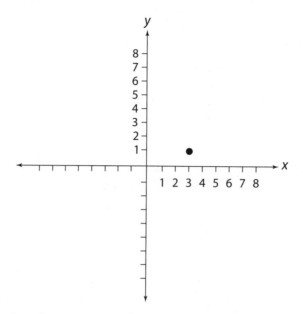

KRISTI: Aren't you supposed to go across 1 and then up 3?

TEACHER: (I am curious to get a sense of how all my students are
             thinking about this and why.) I want to find out what you
             all think about this. If you agree with James's method I
             want you to put your thumbs up. If you agree with Kristi's   570
             method put your thumbs down and if you are not sure put
             your thumbs sideways. (As I look around about a third of the
             group is in each category.)

CARTER: Mr. Elliot, I didn't put my hand up because I don't think it
             matters. I think you can do it either way, and it will work.   575

JACOB: Mr. Borden, my sixth-grade teacher, told us to do it Kristi's
             way. He said that for the x you go across, but I don't know
             why... He just told us to do it that way.

TEACHER: Interesting. So can anyone explain why we would want to do
             it a particular way? Does it matter? (The class is quiet, and by   580
             the looks on their faces, I can tell they are not sure.) So let's
             look at two points, and plot them both ways and see if we can
             sort this out. Let's take James's point (1, 3), and let's also take
             another point (2, 8). If I do it James's way, we go up 1 and over
             3 and then we go up 2 and over 8. With Kristi's way ... I'll use   585
             squares for this ... we go over 1 and up 3 and over 2 and up 8.
             As you look at the dots (James's way) and the squares (Kristi's

way), do you think it makes a difference? I want you to talk in your Think Teams for 3 minutes. Decide if it matters and come up with an argument to explain your thinking. 590

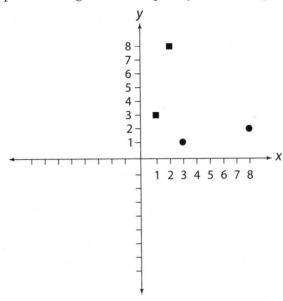

As I walk around, I hear several distinct points of view and, when we come back together, decide to call on a representative from each team.

TEACHER: I heard a couple of different ideas, so let's hear from a couple of different groups. Megan, what did your group decide?

MEGAN: We think it does matter. We drew the graph on a piece of 595 paper and connected the dots. With Kristi's way, the line is steeper than the line with James's way. We don't think a steep line and a flatter line mean the same thing. But, we are not sure why. (Yash's group starts getting real excited.)

YASH: Mr. Elliot, we think we know why. 600

TEACHER: Go ahead.

YASH: From science, we know that time is usually on the *x*-line (he goes up to the board and points to the numbers along the *x*-axis) like 1 minute, 2 minutes, 3 minutes. If we are looking at temperature, then the dots show the temperature going up a 605 little, and the squares show the temperature going up a lot, and both can't be true at the same time.

Karl

GRADE 7, OCTOBER

I put the word *time* under the *x*-axis and *temperature* along the *y*-axis. I also mention that we call these lines the *x*- and *y*-axes. I wait a few moments while students seem to be thinking hard about what Yash has said.

610

TEACHER: Carter, your group was talking about how you did not think it mattered. What is your argument?

CARTER: I think we don't think that anymore. I agree with Yash now. It can't go up a lot and a little at the same time.

TEACHER: In mathematics, there are often agreements made by mathematicians to ensure that there is clear communication. If we do it James's way and people in another class do it Kristi's way, then we may end up with confusion and misinterpret what is happening with the situation represented by the graph. So there is agreement that the *x*-value of an ordered pair, the first value, is telling us to go that many units across the *x*-axis, and the *y*-value is telling us how many units to go up the *y*-axis. As Yash demonstrated, if *x* is time, then it makes sense to count by the *x*-axis units because the *x*-axis is where we recorded the time.

615

620

625

Yash is using a powerful strategy to help him sort things out. He is using an example or context to help him think through the ideas. We have used this strategy before, and here is another example of how helpful it can be.

There is a lot that goes into making sense of the coordinate system. There is so much more that we could discuss as a class. I have a lot of questions about their understanding. What connection do students make between *x* and *y* and the variables of a situation? Do they have reasons for why time should go on the *x*-axis? Do they have a sense of what independent and dependent variables mean? Can they relate the changes in the graph to the changes in data tables or changes in the situation they are graphing? Do they see the graph shows the relationship between two variables or do they simply follow a procedure? Do those students who drew a graph in the shape of a plus sign and those who drew theirs in the shape of an *L* see these as related? What do students understand about the negative values of a coordinate graph?

630

635

640

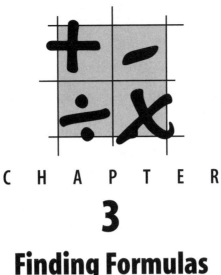

3
Finding Formulas

The functions that appear in Chapters 1 through 5 of this Casebook are of a particular kind. For example, consider a table of values for the Penny Jar context in Abigail's class, Case 7: Start with 7 pennies in the jar, and add 4 each round.

Round Number	Number of Pennies in the Jar
0	7
1	11
2	15
3	19
4	23

For all of the functions we have examined, when the values in the left column increase by 1, the values in the right column increase by a constant amount—in this Penny Jar context, 4. This kind of function is called a *linear function* because its graph is a line.

Another way to look at such a function is to write a formula that, when applied to a value in the left column, gives you the corresponding value in the right column. For example, the formula some of Abigail's students explicate for this Penny Jar context is to multiply the number of the round by 4 and add 7. This formula can also be represented algebraically as $n = (4 \times r) + 7$, where n is the number of pennies in the jar and r is the number of the round.

Students presented in this chapter are all working to find formulas for particular situations. As you begin to read each case, create your own formula, first using words before trying algebraic notation. Then read about what students do as they work on the same task, and consider the teachers' reflections.

C A S E   **10**

Multiple formulas for blue and yellow tiles

Nina

GRADE 8, OCTOBER

Drew is an eighth-grade student with whom I worked for one semester in a class called Math Lab. When students enter this class, I give them a survey that asks them a variety of questions about their perceptions of their math ability. One question asks them to rate their confidence level in math on a scale of 0 to 6: 0 meaning no confidence and 6 meaning complete confidence. I still remember Drew pondering this question for a long time. He said, "I have a lot of confidence in my math ability, but I just don't get the stuff we do in my regular math class." It felt like a contradictory statement at the time, but it started to make more sense to me as I worked with him throughout the semester.

There was one incident that clearly demonstrated Drew's perception of his math confidence. Students were looking at a pattern of blue and yellow tiles—blue tiles in a row with a border of yellow tiles around them. They

5

10

were examining three figures to determine how the pattern of yellow tiles changed as additional blue tiles were added.

 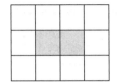 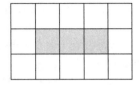

Students had blue and yellow tiles, so they could build more figures and were asked to determine how many yellow tiles would be needed for figures with up to 10 blue tiles. They were also asked to explain the relationship between blue and yellow tiles and to determine how many yellow tiles would be needed to create a pattern containing 50 blue tiles. Finally, they were asked to explain how they could find the number of yellow tiles needed for any number, n, of blue tiles.

Previously, we had done numerous activities looking for patterns in changing figures or situations. So Drew got right to work on this problem. He created a figure with 4 blue tiles and determined that 14 yellow tiles would be needed because, to go from one figure to the next, "you add 1 yellow to the top and bottom horizontal lines. Figure 3 was 12, so this one is 14."

Drew made a table showing the number of yellow tiles needed to build a figure with up to 10 blue tiles.

Number of Blue Tiles	Number of Yellow Tiles
1	8
2	10
3	12
4	14
5	16
6	18
7	20
8	22
9	24
10	26

He described the relationship between blue tiles and yellow tiles. "Every time we go to the next level of blue, there are always 2 more yellow tiles." I asked if he could compare what happens to the blue tiles with what happens to the yellow tiles. He said, "As blue goes up 1, yellow goes up 2."

When we got to the number of yellow tiles needed when the pattern has 50 blue tiles, Drew envisioned the tile arrangements with numbers larger than he could build. "There would be 50 blue tiles in the middle, so there would be 50 yellow tiles on top and on bottom plus 3 yellow tiles on the left and 3 yellow tiles on the right. So, it would be 50×2, which equals 100, plus 6, equals 106 yellow tiles."

	50 yellow tiles	
3	50 blue tiles	3
	50 yellow tiles	

I asked how many yellow tiles would be needed if there were 64 blue tiles in the pattern. He quickly calculated $64 + 64 = 128$, $128 + 6 = 134$. So, 134 yellow tiles would be needed. He did the same for 124 blue tiles: $124 \times 2 + 6 = 254$.

When he was asked to come up with a way to figure out how many yellow tiles would be needed for n blue tiles, he said, "I think $2n + 6$ because the n stands for the number of blue tiles. The 'times 2' is for when you add the 2 yellow tiles for each blue tile. And, the 'plus 6' is for the 2 sides of 3 yellow tiles, which equals 6."

I was truly impressed with Drew's clear explanation of his thinking, but it did not stop there. He then went on to say it could also be $(n + 2)2 + 2$ because the number of blue tiles plus 2 more will give you the number of yellow tiles in the top row. You multiply it by 2 because that will give you the number of yellow tiles in both the top and bottom rows. Finally, you add 2 more yellow tiles because those are the yellow tiles to the right and left of the row of blue tiles.

	"$n + 2$" of yellow tiles	
1	"n" of blue tiles	1
	"$n + 2$" of yellow tiles	

You could also look at it like this: $(n + 2)3 - n$ because you could determine the number of tiles altogether by taking the number of blue tiles, adding 2 more tiles for the total tiles in one row, and then multiply it by 3 to get the total number of tiles from all 3 rows. Finally, you need to subtract n from that number to get rid of the blue tiles. So, what you are left with is the total number of yellow tiles. It would look like this:

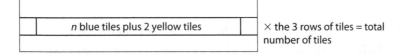

n blue tiles plus 2 yellow tiles $\times$ the 3 rows of tiles = total number of tiles

Total number of tiles – the n number of blue tiles = total number of yellow tiles

I was blown away by the flexibility of Drew's thinking. His ability to move from one model to another and clearly explain why each representation would give the same number of yellow tiles demonstrated strong mathematical reasoning.

When I asked him later why he was successful at this lesson, he replied, "I got into it. I could take the ways the other students were looking at it and do it in new ways." I mentioned to him my memory of his explanation of his confidence level in math from the beginning of the year. He said he tries to figure out the math but sometimes does not understand how to do it. He said that reading explanations from a math book is harder for him, and he understands the math better when he is shown how to do it. I told him he seems to be a visual learner. He replied that he does best when he "sees it" not when he just hears it.

Talking about his experience in regular math class, Drew said it is harder than his other classes; he tries but does not always succeed. I asked, "How can someone help you?" He replied, "Show me an example. Let me watch you do it, and then watch me do it and correct me as I go." I know this is his perception of how he learns math, but I see him as a student who has a strong ability to think through the mathematics on his own. For me, the challenge is to help him tap into his own natural ability.

What's the formula for square borders?

Nancy

How do students discover patterns? Where do they look for them? What
do they see? How do they formulate a rule? I asked myself these questions
after giving my students a problem similar to one that appeared on their
statewide test. Students were given a group of 4 figures with this description: The first figure is a square border made up of 3 smaller squares on
each side; the second figure shows 4 squares on each side; the third figure,
5 squares on each side; the fourth figure, 6 squares on each side. Students
were told that the pattern continues in this way and were asked to respond
to a set of prompts about the figures.

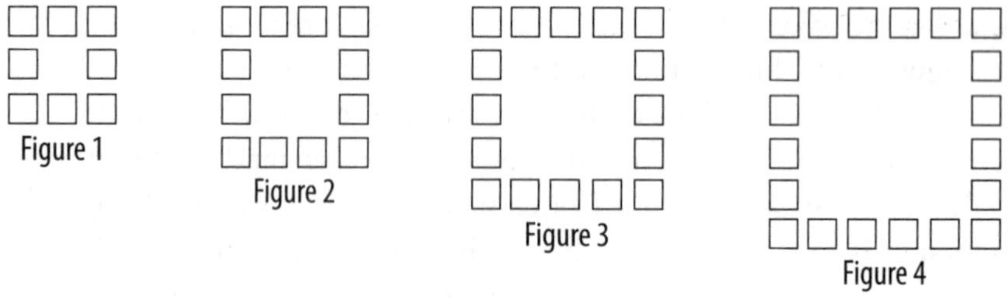

Figure 1

Figure 2

Figure 3

Figure 4

1. Draw Figure 5.

2. Determine how many tiles would be needed for Figure 7.

3. Make a table for the first 10 figures showing the relationship between
   each figure number and the number of tiles in the figure.

4. Find a relationship between the figure number and the number of tiles
   used.

Students were given tiles to help them construct the figures. While
working in pairs, all students were able to draw Figure 5 and determine
the number of tiles needed for Figure 7. Most did so by creating Figure 6
first and then building on Figure 6 to make Figure 7. Some confusion arose
when they worked on item 3. They were not sure what was meant by a

table. So, I drew a table for the class to look at and labeled the left column "Figure Number" and the right-hand column "Number of Tiles." Showing students this first step seemed to provide enough support for them to | 105
complete the table.

In response to item 4, students explained that 4 more tiles were added to the previous figure to generate the next. "It went up 4 tiles each time." The table was useful to them in seeing this pattern.

Figure Number	Number of Tiles
1	8
2	12
3	16
4	20
5	24
6	28
7	32
8	36
9	40
10	44

The challenge came when they were asked to find the number of tiles | 110
they would need to build the 50th figure. Elaine explained her group's thinking:

ELAINE: We multiplied 50 × 4 and came up with 200 tiles.

TEACHER: What does the 50 stand for?

ELAINE: It is the 50th figure. | 115

TEACHER: What does the 4 stand for?

ELAINE: It is the 4 tiles that are added to the figure.

I asked the students to go back to Figure 4 and apply the same strategy to that figure. The students multiplied 4 × 4 and came up with 16, but they knew Figure 4 had 20 tiles, not 16. One student responded, "That's weird." | 120

They also applied their rule to Figure 8 (8 × 4 = 32) and found that their answer was off by 4 again; the number of tiles was supposed to be 36. I suggested they think about why they were off by 4.

One group of students actually continued the table all the way up to the 50th figure by adding 4 each time.

CAROLINE: We took each figure and added 4 to get the next figure. We did this all the way up and when we got the 49th figure, that was 200 tiles. Figure 50 was 204.

Elaine commented that if we took the 50 × 4 and added 4 more, we would get 204 tiles for the 50th figure. Students applied this process to Figures 4 and 8 and saw the new formula gave them the numbers in the table. Caroline said that adding 4 made sense because that is what she and Ivan did to create the number of tiles needed for all the figures up to Figure 50. They added 4 each time.

I wanted students to connect the arithmetic they were doing (50 × 4) to the structure of the square tiles, so I posed a question about that.

TEACHER: Why do we multiply the figure number by 4?

NATHAN: Because we keep adding 4 each time.

I was wondering if students were seeing the connection between adding 4 tiles each time and the multiplication statement. Were they thinking about continuing the pattern they saw as they looked down the column in the table, or were they thinking about using the figure number and working across the table? I could not tell from Nathan's answer.

I asked students to look at the shape of the figure. Leila responded that it had 4 sides. Although Leila's observation was bringing more meaning to the problem, no one picked up on her idea. I asked students to look at the number of tiles in each side of each figure. They noticed that the sides grew by 1 from one figure to the next. We added a third column to the table and labeled the column "Number of Tiles in a Side."

Nathan stated that he noticed that if, as in Figure 1, you multiplied the number of tiles in its side (3) by the number of sides (4), you get 12, which is the number of tiles in Figure 2, not Figure 1. This works for all the figures. When you multiply the number of tiles in a side of a figure by the 4 sides, you get the number of tiles in the next figure.

We were close to the connection I wanted my students to make, but the class period was coming to an end. Students had come up with a rule for finding the number of tiles for any figure: Multiply the number of the figure by 4 and add 4. To conclude the lesson, I asked students to figure out the number of tiles needed for Figure 101. All students were able to determine that it would be (101 × 4) + 4, or 408 tiles. However, it was clear they could not explain *why* it was the figure number multiplied by 4, plus 4.

Although the class was coming to an end, one student, Kevin, continued to pursue the 50th figure pattern. I asked him to refocus on the number of tiles on the side of the figure and what happened when the sides are added together. He, too, noticed that the number of tiles on the side of a figure was 2 more than the figure number. I asked him to use either words or symbols to write an expression for determining the number of tiles in any figure. He came up with the following: $4(n + 2) - 4 =$ the number of tiles in a figure in which n is the figure number. He added 2 to n because the number of tiles on the side is 2 more than the figure number, a pattern he noticed. He multiplied it by 4 because there are 4 sides in the figure. Finally, he subtracted 4 because it eliminated the duplication of adding the corners. He had been learning the Distributive Property in his regular math class, so I asked him to apply the property for this problem. He multiplied through to get $4n + 8 - 4 = 4n + 4$. This is what my other students had come up with, but they did not have a sense of how numbers and operations in the expression connected to the figures.

C A S E   **12**

Finding strategies

Jesse

GRADES 4 AND 5, MAY

I work as a math coach. While my primary focus is helping teachers deepen their understanding of math content and supporting them as they work to implement a new math curriculum, I often work with children to help them develop problem-solving strategies. The other day, one teacher invited me to work with students in her Grades 4 and 5 learning disabled classroom. She stated that the children had difficulty working with

patterns and using information embedded in a problem to effectively
solve the problem. She asked if I would sit with a few individual students
as they worked on the following problem:

 In the pattern below,

- 5 blocks are needed to form a space the size of 1 square.

- 6 blocks are needed to form a space the size of 2 squares.

- 7 blocks are needed to form a space the size of 3 squares.

 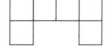 

If the pattern continues in this way, what size is the space that is
formed by 12 blocks?

The first student I worked with was Shaquin, a fifth grader. He describes himself as someone who likes math and is a good problem solver.
At the beginning of our work, he stated, "I'm a good thinker."

He began by reading the problem, but stopped almost immediately and
asked, "What's this word?" He pointed to the word *pattern*.

TEACHER: *Pattern*.

SHAQUIN: What's a pattern?

TEACHER: A necklace sometimes has a pattern.

I drew the following patterns on a piece of paper:

○□○□○□   ○□○○□□○○○□□□

SHAQUIN: The first one is a pattern; it goes round, square, round,
            square. But, the second one changes.

TEACHER: If you were to add beads to the first necklace, you would add
            round, square. What would you add to the other necklace so
            it also continues a pattern?

SHAQUIN: You could start over. Or, maybe you could add round, round,
            round, round, then 4 squares.

TEACHER: Either one would work. One pattern repeats. One keeps
            changing, but in a regular way.

SHAQUIN: (Turning back to the block structures) These patterns aren't the same. They change.

TEACHER: Does anything else change?

SHAQUIN: This is missing 1 square (pointing to the space in the first figure that would complete the rectangle). This is missing 2 squares (pointing to the second figure). This is missing 3 squares (pointing to the third figure). One more each time.

TEACHER: Shaquin, can you figure out how many squares would fit into the space if you used 8 blocks?

Shaquin quickly built a structure with cubes but used 10 cubes. He counted each cube by 1 and said, "Take out 2. 4, 4 squares missing."

TEACHER: What if you used 12 cubes, how many spaces would there be then?

SHAQUIN: 8

TEACHER: How do you know?

SHAQUIN: I used my head. I counted 1, 2, 3, 4. You have four more cubes, so you have four more spaces.

Shaquin wrote out the following table and showed how you can count on 4 from 8 in the top row to get to 12 cubes, and you count on 4 from 4 in the bottom row to get to 8 spaces.

5	6	7	8	9	10	11	12
1	2	3	4	5	6	7	8

TEACHER: How can you check to see if you are right?

SHAQUIN: Build it. (He then takes cubes and counts 1, 2, 3, ... 10.) 2 more. I was right, it was 8.

TEACHER: Let's go back and think about what you said about how the pattern goes.

SHAQUIN: It's easy. (Pointing to the table) 5 minus 1 is 4, 6 minus 2 is 4, 7 minus 3 is 4. This one is 12 take away 8 equals 4. The legs stay the same, but the middle changes. It's always 4 to make the legs.

215

220

225

230

235

Jesse

GRADES 4 AND 5, MAY

Shaquin first built his model and counted by 1s, examining the number patterns to answer the questions. At the end of our discussion, he talked about how the numbers are related to the structure of the figures.

Another student, Brian, also a fifth grader, first thought about the structure of the figures when he was working out the number patterns.

BRIAN: Each one has a pattern. See, this one (he points to the 5-cube structure), it's 3 plus 3.

TEACHER: What do you mean?

BRIAN: Right there. 1, 2, 3. (He breaks the structure into 2 sets—the first set forming an upside-down capital *L*, the second, a lowercase *l*—and points to the empty space.) If you added 1 here, it would be 3 and 3.

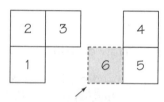

BRIAN: They look like bridges. Each bridge gets bigger by 2s.

He then lined up each "bridge" one behind the other.

BRIAN: Oh, it's bigger by 1. This part gets bigger (touching the cross beam). You could count the squares in the space by making the bridges into rectangles.

TEACHER: Terrific. How many spaces with 8 cubes?

BRIAN: 4, because 4 plus 4 is 8.

Finding Formulas

Jesse

TEACHER:	9 cubes?
BRIAN:	9 equals 5 because the 8 is 4, and 9 is 5.	260
TEACHER:	Can I challenge you? How many spaces when there are 12 cubes?
BRIAN:	8
TEACHER:	How did you figure that so quickly?
BRIAN:	Easy, 9 is 5, 10 is 6, 11 is 7, 12 is 8. I counted those spaces in my head.	265

Tanikua is a fourth grader and one of only two girls in this class. She was excited to begin working and said, "I have a lot of imagination." I wondered what understanding she would bring to her work.

After looking at the drawings and the cube models the boys had been working with, Tanikua picked up the models and started to combine all the cubes into one structure. She then pointed to the drawings and said, "It looks like a chart."

TEACHER:	Can you tell me more about what you are noticing?
TANIKUA:	They all stand on 2 cubes on each side. They're not the same size, and they're different colors. Different shapes, too.
TEACHER:	What do you mean?
TANIKUA:	This one's bigger (she points at the 7-cube structure). This one's medium (6). This one is small (5). They have empty spaces in the middle. 5 cubes—1 space, 6 cubes—2 spaces, 7 cubes—3 spaces.

I asked her to write down what she was saying. She immediately organized her observations into a table:

5	1
6	2
7	3

TEACHER:	If we build one with 8 cubes?

| TANIKUA: | How many spaces would there be? I think there would be 6 spaces. | 285 |

TEACHER: How could you check your answer?

Without replying, Tanikua took cubes and began to build.

TANIKUA: There are 4 spaces.

She then added 8 and 4 to her table. | 290

TANIKUA: That's weird. It goes 1, 2, 3, 4, and then 5, 6, 7, 8.

TEACHER: Could you use your table to figure how many spaces there would be with 12 cubes?

Tanikua picked up the cubes and started to arrange them. She tried a couple of different shapes until she built a structure with 2 cubes on each | 295 end, joined by a row of cubes across the top.

TANIKUA: 8. It looks like a cell phone.

She then carefully added this new information to her table but made no comment about it.

I was pleased with how the students in this class worked on solving the | 300 pattern problem. While many of them had difficulty reading the problem, and some, like Shaquin, could only begin working after discussing what a pattern is, they brought their ingenuity, images, and number skills to bear as they addressed the questions posed to them.

Shaquin, Brian, and Tanikua were able to observe elements of the | 305 patterns and to make predictions based on what they were seeing. They investigated by recreating the models, making references to everyday objects—bridges, tables, cell phones, legs—and by finding out how the cubes and spaces were related to each other. They were able to use that informa- tion to anticipate changes as the pattern grew and to justify their answers. | 310

In the initial stages of his work, Shaquin built models of the cube pat- tern that allowed him to see the embodied information numerically. His final response, "It's easy," rested on models that enabled him to discover that there is a consistent difference of 4 between the number of cubes in the figure and number of cubes that would fit in the space. | 315

Brian decomposed the figures differently than Shaquin but also noted the relationship between the number of cubes and the size of the space. The image of a bridge helped him to see that the number of cubes and the size of the space both increased by 1 each step.

Tanikua's observations about the pattern models are accurate and to
the point. She states that they "look like a chart" and later takes beginning
steps to create a table to organize the information. Although the table does
not seem to directly help her solve the problem, her conversation about it
allows us to notice that she is at the beginning of learning to see numerical
relationships in a table form.

C A S E   **13**

Henrietta's roost

Samantha

GRADE 1, MAY

Throughout the past several months, my professional-development
group has been discussing the idea of generalization and early algebraic
thinking. I have watched and listened carefully as my kindergarten
students have wrestled with some ideas about odd and even numbers
and about the predictable nature of patterns. As I have recorded their
thinking, I have often wondered if there might be a time when I would
observe students exploring the usefulness of algebraic expressions or
formulas. Much to my surprise and delight I think I saw a glimmer of
this last Friday afternoon.

As part of my teaching responsibilities, I team-teach in a first-grade
classroom when my kindergarten students are not in session. This time is
primarily reserved for math workshop. Often we try to connect the mathematical ideas we are working on with other units the children are study-
ing. Currently the first graders have an incubator set up in their classroom
to aid them in a study of the life cycles of chickens. They have also been
to a local farm to see how chickens are raised. Using this as a jumping-off
point, my teaching partner and I posed the following question to her first-
grade class:

> In the chicken coop the hens roost in a line.
> Each hen has her own roost.

> Henrietta's roost is in the middle.
> It is the 7th roost.
> How many hens are in the line?

We initially read the problem aloud with the class, and then children worked in groups to solve it. We asked them not only to think about a solution but also to describe their strategies for solving the problem. It was clear from the start that Diane and Norman had each arrived at a solution and were quick to share their respective strategies with their peers. Time was provided for both thinking and sharing as a whole group. Then children were given a second problem identical to the first except that the ordinal position Henrietta occupied in the line was changed. We reminded students that in each case Henrietta remained in the middle.

By making this change in the problem, my partner and I hoped we might see children begin to generalize their strategies. Many children used cubes to work through the problem. When asked to share their work, they would offer the solution and then, in an attempt to share their strategy, would say something like ... Henrietta is 7th (putting their finger on the 7th Unifix cube). She is in the middle (again holding their finger on the cube in the same position as if to demonstrate that this place was also the middle). For most children, this was as far as the explanation would go. For both Diane and Norman, something very different happened—they were very clear about their strategies. I found some time to meet with each of them individually to talk about their work.

I started with Diane whose written work is seen on the facing page.

TEACHER: Diane, I see that you worked on the problem in which Henrietta was 11th in line. Can you tell me how you solved the problem?

Name **Diane** _____ Date _____

Chicken Coop

In the chicken coop the hens roost in a line. Each hen has her own roost. Henrietta's roost is in the middle. It is **11**th. How many hens are in the line? 21

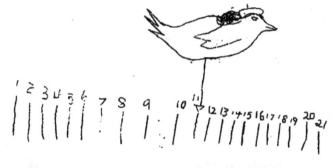

yes! Your recording shows clearly how you solved this problem

---

DIANE: I know she's the 11th one. So, I made 11 little lines, and I made Henrietta the 11th one. (She pointed to the drawing of a hen on her recording sheet.) I saw it's 10 right before her (pointing to the 10 lines drawn to the left of the hen) and I counted 10 on the other side (pointing to the 10 lines drawn to the right of the hen).

TEACHER: Why did you do this?

375

DIANE: Because I knew she had to be in the middle, and it had to be   380
an even number on each side.

TEACHER: How did you know it had to be an even number on each
side?

DIANE: 10 here (pointing to the 10 lines before the hen) and 10 here   385
(pointing to the 10 lines after the hen). She's in the middle.
It wouldn't be an even number if you counted her. What I
should have said is that it had to be the *same* number on each
side of her.

TEACHER: Will it always be the same number on each side of her?

DIANE: Yes.   390

At this, Diane turned to a second recording sheet she had and counted
the 5 lines on each side of Henrietta that she had drawn showing Henrietta
6th in line and in the middle.

Name __Diane_____ Date _____

Chicken Coop

In the chicken coop the hens roost in a line. Each
hen has her own roost. Henrietta's roost is in the
middle. It is __6__th. How many hens are in the line? | 11 |

I see   5 + 1 + 5 = 11

Nice Job!!

| DIANE: | If it was this number, say 5, on this side, it would have to be the same number on the other side. | 395 |

TEACHER: What about every time?

With this Diane looked confused.

TEACHER: Let's try another one. What if Henrietta is 8th and in the middle?

| DIANE: | 15 (This was done very quickly and without paper and pencil.) | 400 |

TEACHER: How did you get that?

DIANE: I took away Henrietta from the 8 and I had 7, and so I put 7 on the other side.

| TEACHER: | Try 15. | 405 |

DIANE: 29

TEACHER: How did you get this one so fast?

DIANE: 15 take away 1 for Henrietta, I get 14, and so 14 plus 14 equals 28, then I add 1 is 29.

| TEACHER: | You seem to have a strategy that works for solving this problem. Will it always work? | 410 |

DIANE: Yes, I think so.

TEACHER: What would it take to convince you that it would always work?

| DIANE: | Do it a really lot of times and if they all come out right! | 415 |

Diane spoke this last statement with conviction. I was so excited by her thinking and her ability to articulate her thought process. In my mind I could see two equations taken together, something like $x - 1 = y$ and $y + y + 1 = n$, where x is Henrietta's position in line, y is the number of hens on either side of Henrietta, and n is the total number of hens.

I realize that Diane did not have the vocabulary or symbols to write these equations, yet somehow she had so clearly defined the steps she used each time. Is this the beginning of algebraic thinking? Were other children doing something similar but without the ability to articulate it yet? What experiences will Diane need to be convinced that the steps she takes each time can always solve this problem, regardless of the ordinal position Henrietta sits in the line?

While my mind was still buzzing, I asked Norman if he would talk with me.

TEACHER: I was wondering if you could tell me more about your work. I see that you wrote, "I know that 10 + 10 = 20, but it's the same thing as when she was 7th."

> I now that 10+10 =20 but it's the sam thing a whenshe was 7th

NORMAN: She's 10th. I know 10 and 10 is 20, so it's 19 because it's the same as the 7th one. 7 plus 7 is 14, but it doesn't work that way. I know it's 13 because 6 on each side. Because if it was 7, there isn't one in the middle of 7 plus 7.

TEACHER: It seems like you have a strategy. Does it always work?

NORMAN: I don't know, but I think so.

TEACHER: Let's try another one. What if Henrietta is 15th?

NORMAN: Isn't 15 plus 15, 30? (I wasn't sure if Norman was asking me or just thinking aloud. I waited and he continued.) So 15 plus 15 is 30, minus 1 is 29.

Norman began to make little lines on a piece of paper and then stopped and got a basket of cubes and snapped together 29 cubes.

TEACHER: What are you doing?

NORMAN: I'm checking. See I have 1, 2, 3 ...

Norman counted from 1 to 15 (left to right along the line of cubes) and placed his finger on the 15th cube. He held his finger at this spot and then started counting again, only this time he started at the 15th spot and called that 1 and then counted each of the remaining cubes.

NORMAN: See, there are 14 on this side (pointing to the cubes to the left of his finger) plus that cube, and 14 on this side (pointing to the cubes to the right of his finger). And 1 in the middle. It couldn't be 15 on each side, there wouldn't be a middle.

TEACHER: I'm a little confused. How do you know there wouldn't be a middle? 455

NORMAN: See, if it was 15 and 15 then there isn't one in the middle, so I know it's 1 less.

TEACHER: What do you mean 1 less?

NORMAN: See, if I have 15 on this side (pointing to half of his stick of cubes), then I have to have 15 on this side. But then there isn't a middle. 460

With this Norman broke his stick of cubes so that one tower had 15 cubes and the other tower had 14 cubes. He then added 1 more cube to the tower of 14. 465

NORMAN: See, now they are even. 15 plus 15 is 30, but there isn't a middle, so I take 1 away.

Norman proceeded to break off the cube he had just added.

TEACHER: Now I see. Do you think this strategy will work every time?

NORMAN: Yeah ... 470

Norman did not sound very convinced.

TEACHER: You don't sound too sure. What would it take to convince you?

NORMAN: Well, I think I would have to try it a lot. Do I have to do that?

Norman had a panicky look. I assured him that he did not have to try 475
more problems and thanked him for talking with me. As he walked away
I was struck that even with his level of confidence he, like Diane, was not
sure it would always work but that trying more problems would help. I
was struck by how familiar this felt. When have students done enough to
develop trust in numbers and strategies? 480

Even if the element of "always" was not present for either Diane or
Norman, I was very impressed with their respective ways of generalizing
a strategy. Again, looking back at Norman's work I can see the buds of
algebraic thought and perhaps a formula. Was he not saying that $2x - 1$

was how he arrived at his solution, if x was the ordinal position Henrietta held in the line? Didn't Norman see that doubling the number was too much because then there would not be a middle? Didn't he seem to see the importance of taking one away in order to allow for that spot? Like Diane, Norman did not have the vocabulary or symbols, but can't you hear it in his thinking? I think I can.

4

Comparing Linear Functions

CASE 14	The crawling crayfish	Lydia	Grade 4, October
CASE 15	Can Bolar catch up?	Michelle	Grade 3, March
CASE 16	Collecting bottles	Nadia	Grade 4, January

Consider the following Penny Jar situations:

Emad starts with 20 pennies in his jar and adds 15 each round.

Micah starts with 10 pennies in his jar and adds 5 each round.

Juan starts with 10 pennies in his jar and adds 20 each round.

With the two pieces of information about each child's collection of pennies, can we know who will have more as they proceed with their rounds? Emad starts out with more than both Micah and Juan. Will Emad continue to have more than Micah? Juan adds more pennies than both Emad and Micah. Even though they start with the same amount, after the first round, Juan will have more than Micah. What about Emad? Will Juan ever catch up with him? When? And what happens after that?

In the cases presented in this chapter, students address similar questions in other contexts. In Case 14, fourth graders predict the outcome of a race between two crayfish. In Case 15, third graders consider a group of children on a fantasy planet who accumulate an allowance of magic marbles at different rates. In Case 16, fourth graders work to represent a similar situation (students accumulating bottles). In all three cases, the linear functions the students are working with can be compared because students are given the two key pieces of information for each function: the starting number and the rate of increase.

Throughout each case, students work to create representations of the scenarios they are investigating. Some are learning about conventional representations, such as tables and graphs, but others generate less standard representations. As you read, work to understand how each of the representations provides a tool for students' thinking.

C A S E   14

The crawling crayfish

GRADE 4, OCTOBER

We had recently finished a science unit that used crayfish in an engaging way to help children learn about the Scientific Method. As part of this unit, children conducted crayfish "races," collected data about their speed, and graphed the results. I decided to pose a math problem that would harness the children's "crayfish enthusiasm" and allow me to investigate their thinking about patterns of change.

I presented the following problem to the children:

> Big Claw, the crayfish, challenged Flicker to a 60 cm race. Because Big Claw is much larger, he offered to give Flicker a 10 cm head start. Flicker agreed and the race began. After 5 seconds, Big Claw had crawled 6 cm, and Flicker had crawled 4 cm. If they continue at this rate, who do you predict will win the race?

5

10

Comparing Linear Functions

I was interested in exploring the range of responses to the following:

- What predictions will the children make about which crayfish wins the race?

- What will they base their predictions on?

- How will the children represent the actions modeled in the race?

- What patterns will they notice?

- Will they use the patterns to identify which crayfish wins the race before the race is over? If so, how?

- How will the children use each crayfish's speed to determine the outcome of the race?

Predictions centered around three different features of the race. The salient feature for some of the children was the narrative style. These children based their predictions on what might happen in a story rather than thinking about the mathematics involved.

ZEB: After Flicker has gone 4 centimeters, he gets tired so he goes slower.

BRENDA: Big Claw may run out of breath because he's so big.

A few children made predictions based both on their observations of the crayfish (the actual crayfish in our study) and the math involved.

NORA: Big Claw is longer and Flicker is shorter, so Big Claw will still get to the finish line sooner.

Most children had some sense that the rate the crayfish crawled remained constant, and based their predictions on this knowledge. Because the winner was not readily apparent to the children before they began keeping track of the data, I knew there would probably be some disagreement about the winner.

GIOVANNI: I think Big Claw will win because he goes farther every time.

SHAWNA: (holding her hands out) Big Claw goes this much every time. Every 5 seconds, Flicker doesn't go as far.

AVERY: Flicker will win because he's already 10 centimeters more. Big Claw would have to go at least 10 centimeters each time.

JOSIE: I think it will be a tie because since Big Claw goes farther each time and Flicker goes only 4 [centimeters]; I think Big Claw will catch up.

TYSON: Flicker will win. I did it in my head. I added 4 centimeters and 10 centimeters and that makes 14 centimeters. 14 plus 4 is 18. Then I added 0 plus 6 for Big Claw and got 6. 6 plus 6 is 12 so Big Claw has only gone 12 centimeters.

LIANE: I predict it will be closer at the beginning, but Big Claw will go faster and every 5 seconds he will get 2 centimeters closer. So Big Claw will win by a lot.

With the children eager to prove their hypotheses, I sent them off in teams to solve the problem. Most children began by using paper and pencil to create the track in the form of a time line. On this track, they recorded the two crayfish jumps of 4 or 6 centimeters.

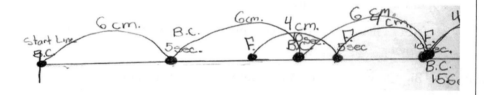

For some of the children who used this strategy, it was difficult to keep track of the distance and the time simultaneously so their representations were either incomplete or incorrect. But some children (such as Melanie, a part of whose work is shown above) were able to keep track and could read quite a bit of information from their representations.

Some children chose to create a more concrete model of the problem using base-10 rods to represent increments of 10 centimeters. Using objects such as erasers and pencils, they kept track of each crayfish's progress.

A few children created race diagrams that separated the progress of the two crayfish and were able to use their representations to accurately predict the winner of the race at the 60-centimeter mark.

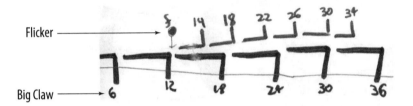

ANGELA: They are tied when they get to 30 centimeters and then Big Claw gets ahead. He's going to win because he goes 6 cm and Flicker only goes 4.

Only one child, Tyson, chose to use a table to keep track of the information. I planned to ask him to share his table the following day during our follow-up discussion so that other children could interpret the race more clearly.

The next day, Tyson shared the table he made by recreating it on chart paper at our math meeting place. I hoped that once the information was presented in this format, the children would begin to notice and comment on the patterns they saw.

Handwritten table titled "Flicker" and "Big Claw"

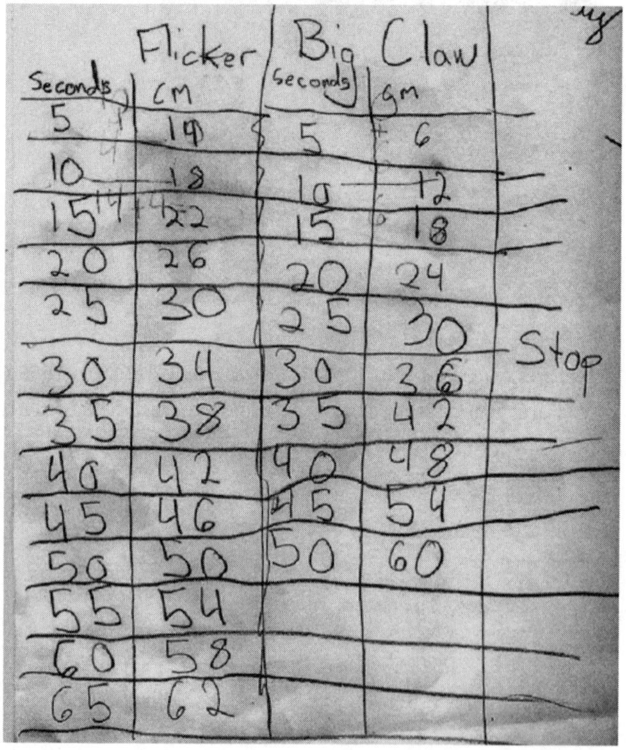

Flicker Seconds	cm	Big Claw Seconds	gm
5	14	5	6
10	18	10	12
15	22	15	18
20	26	20	24
25	30	25	30 — Stop
30	34	30	36
35	38	35	42
40	42	40	48
45	46	45	54
50	50	50	60
55	54		
60	58		
65	62		

TYSON: First I made a column for the seconds for Flicker and the centimeters. Then next to it, I made the same thing for Big Claw. I started with 14 for Flicker because I had to add 10 centimeters to his for the head start. I wrote *stop* after 25 seconds because I knew that Big Claw would win since they were tied, and he goes 2 centimeters faster than Flicker.

CARL: If they're tied at half the race, since Flicker got a 10 centimeter head start, then Big Claw has to win by 10 centimeters.

Carl knows that the 10-centimeter head start will be balanced somewhere in the end because they are tied at the halfway mark.

I wanted to push the children to think about the patterns in the difference between the two crayfish's distances. I reminded them of Liane's comment from yesterday about when the crayfish would be close to each other.

TEACHER: So yesterday, Liane was thinking about whether the crayfish would be close together at the beginning of the race and then far apart. What do you think now, Liane?

LIANE:	I see a pattern. In the beginning, they are far apart. Then they get closer.	
CARL:	Then they get far apart. That's what happened to mine (pointing to the crayfish track he had drawn)!	
TEACHER:	How far apart are they at first?	100
JACKIE:	Look! First they're 8 apart, then 6, then 4. It keeps going down by 2 until they are tied. (I record the differences up to 25 seconds next to the table as Jackie says them.)	
SHAWNA:	Then it goes back up, but this time Big Claw is ahead! (I continue to record the differences as Shawna recites them.)	105

Flicker		Big Claw		Difference cm
Seconds	cm	Seconds	cm	
5	10	5	6	8
10	18	10	12	6
15	22	15	18	4
20	26	20	24	2
25	30	25	30	0
30	34	30	36 Stop	2
35	38	35	42	4
40	42	40	48	6
45	46	45	54	8
50	50	50	60	10
55	54			
60	58			
65	62			

ADRIANNE:	It's kind of like these are negative numbers (pointing to the differences between the distances at the top of the table), and these are the regular numbers (pointing to the differences at the bottom of the table). They [the numbers at the top of the table] count down, but they are really getting more because Big Claw is getting closer. Once they reach 0 ...

Chapter 4 • Case 14

STEVEN: They're tied!

ADRIANNE: They start going back up.

TEACHER: Why do they keep going up or down by 2?

NORA: I get it! It's because Big Claw is always going 2 centimeters faster.   115

The lesson continued as children used the table to identify how long it took Big Claw to finish the race. They used what they had learned about decimals in our previous unit to proudly note that Flicker would cross the finish line at 62.5 seconds, 12.5 seconds behind Big Claw.   120

C A S E   15

Can Bolar catch up?

Michelle

GRADE 3, MARCH

My class has been working on a set of activities based on a fantasy story in which, for one month each year, children receive daily allowances of Magic Marbles. Some of the children begin the month with Magic Marbles that have been saved from the previous year. Students are asked to look for patterns in how the children accumulate their marbles, compare the   125
total amount of marbles that each child has, and describe what is happening over the month.

In the beginning, most of my students thought the child with the most marbles at the start of the month would, of course, be the winner at the end of the month! For example, Zupin started out with 60 marbles while   130
Franick had only 30 marbles from the previous year. Everyone wanted to be Zupin!

As they began to pay attention to how many marbles the children had each day, they were able to see the impact of receiving more marbles each night. That is, they began to pay attention to the different rates of change.   135

In one lesson, the students' task was to track the number of marbles that Franick and Bolar would collect over a month, given the following information.

Franick begins with 30 and gets 3 marbles each night.

Bolar has no marbles at all at the beginning but gets 5 marbles each night.

At first most students thought Franick would have the most marbles at the end of the month because she starts with 30 and Bolar starts with none. However, after they had filled out the table for the 30 days, we had a discussion about the number of marbles each child had collected.

I put the table showing the number of marbles collected during the first two weeks on the overhead projector.

	Day	Franick	Bolar
	Beginning	30	0
Week 1	Day 1	33	5
	Day 2	36	10
	Day 3	39	15
	Day 4	42	20
	Day 5	45	25
	Day 6	48	30
	Day 7	51	35
Week 2	Day 8	54	40
	Day 9	57	45
	Day 10	60	50
	Day 11	63	55
	Day 12	66	60
	Day 13	69	65
	Day 14	72	70

TEACHER: OK, great. The whole time we're looking at these, you really want to see what you notice about these numbers. This is really important right now. So put on your math hats and look at these numbers. Look at Week 1 and Week 2. The first

	thing I want you to think about is what you notice about Franick's and Bolar's marbles. What do you notice about the numbers of marbles? Do you see any patterns?
DYLAN:	They both ... Bolar really starts catching up by the end of the second week.
TEACHER:	Dylan is saying that Bolar really starts to catch up during the end of the second week. That's what he notices when he starts to look at these numbers. Keep going.
DYLAN:	Because as we ... Bolar gets ahead by 2. He keeps going closer and closer by 2.
TEACHER:	Oh, OK, so he's getting closer and closer to Franick?
DYLAN:	Yeah.
TEACHER:	OK. Who else notices something? Noni?
NONI:	With Franick's it goes 3, 6, 9, and then on Bolar's 5, 10, 15, 20. And then it's a pattern because there's 3s and 5s.
TEACHER:	The pattern is Franick goes by 3s and Bolar goes by 5s?
NONI:	Um-hmm.
TEACHER:	OK, Kevin.
KEVIN:	After this tie with Franick and Bolar on Day 15, they both get 75. Then Bolar starts getting more marbles than Franick. On Day 16, Franick has 78, and Bolar has 80.

Kevin was looking into Week 3, which was not yet posted on the overhead. However, because we all saw what happened on Day 14, everyone could easily calculate what happened on Days 15 and 16.

TEACHER:	OK, why do you think that is? Why do you think once they're even on Day 15, that Bolar gets ahead?
KEVIN:	Because Bolar gets 5 marbles and Franick gets 3 marbles.
TEACHER:	How many days did it take them to get to the same amount? Caroline?
CAROLINE:	It took them 15 days.

TEACHER:	It took them 15 days to get to the same amount. Good. OK, we just described some patterns that we see. Does anyone else see any more patterns they can share?
NICK:	In the second week, it's up by 14, 12, 10, 8 ...

Nick has calculated the difference between Franick's and Bolar's marbles on Days 8, 9, 10, and 11.

TEACHER:	Oh, so it's going 14, 12, 10, so it's getting closer by ...
NICK:	8, 6, 4, 2.
TEACHER:	(Referring to the table on the overhead) Nick notices that the difference here (pointing to Day 8) is 14, the difference here (pointing to Day 9) is 12, the difference here (pointing to Day 10) is 10. Does anyone else notice that? The distance between the numbers is 8 different here, 6 different here; he notices that it's 4 different here ...
NICK:	Then 2.
TEACHER:	So as the days go up, what is happening to the distance between the numbers?
NICK:	It's going down by 2.
TEACHER:	Nick, that was an excellent observation. Did anyone else notice that?
DIANA:	I noticed that Bolar at the end, it's more higher than Franick.
TEACHER:	OK, so Diana jumped ahead to the end of the month and noticed that on Day 30, Bolar is higher than Franick. Jose, did you notice something? Are you going to stay on Week 1 or 2, or are you going ahead?
JOSE:	The top one and the bottom, mine is like Diana's, but in the beginning I think everyone was thinking that Franick had more because in the beginning Bolar had less. And then as the weeks passed, he got more and more.

Students had already started to discuss what happened in the rest of the month, so I put up the rest of the table.

Michelle

GRADE 3, MARCH

	Day 15	75	75
	Day 16	78	80
	Day 17	81	85
Week 3	Day 18	84	90
	Day 19	87	95
	Day 20	90	100
	Day 21	93	105
	Day 22	96	110
	Day 23	99	115
	Day 24	102	120
Week 4	Day 25	105	125
	Day 26	108	130
	Day 27	111	135
	Day 28	114	140
Week 5	Day 29	117	145
	Day 30	120	150

TEACHER: (Pointing to chart) When you made your own tables, did you notice the distance up here between the numbers? Did anybody notice? If this one [Day 22] is 14 different, what do you think this one [Day 23] would be? If we're going...look at this pattern going backward. They're 2 different here. What do you think this one [Day 23] might be?

STUDENTS: 16

TEACHER: What do you think the next one [Day 24] might be?

STUDENTS: 18, 20, 22, ...

TEACHER: Are we right? Is that the difference? Interesting. So they started out, if we keep going, 22, ...

STUDENTS: 24, 26, and 28.

215

220

Comparing Linear Functions

Michelle

GRADE 3, MARCH

TEACHER: Don't forget, before they started, Franick had 30 and Bolar had 0. What is the difference there?

JOSE: 30

TEACHER: Great. What happened at the end of the month? Bolar was ahead. I need an explanation for that. Wouldn't you expect that Franick would be the winner because she started out with 30 marbles she saved from last year, but Bolar had spent all of his before the beginning of the month?

BAREED: It's because he was counting by more marbles. He counts by more marbles instead of just 3. He counts by 5.

TEACHER: OK, what about Kyle? You had a good idea.

KYLE: Franick counted by 3s, and then Bolar got more because he counted by 5s, and then Franick got 3 so Bolar catches up.

TEACHER: What if we were only doing it for 2 weeks? What if we weren't going to do it for the whole 30 days? What if we were only going to collect marbles for 14 days? Would Bolar have had a chance to catch up then, Caroline?

CAROLINE: No, because he only had 70, and Franick had 72. Bolar just needed like 5 more to be ahead of Franick.

TEACHER: OK, does anyone else have any explanations for why this happened? Noni?

NONI: Well, Bolar spent his, and he's not getting more, he's getting less. So say he got less because he spent his, because if you go back in the first story it says he spent his, so that's all he spent. And then he got more so that's how he got less money and then he went ahead by 5.

TEACHER: So he got more each night than ... Dylan?

DYLAN: He won because by the second week he's only down by 2. Franick is counting by 3s, which is 2 less than 5s.

CAROLINE: I knew that 5 was more than 3, so I knew that Bolar would be ahead of Franick because 5 is 2 more than 3.

Collecting bottles

Nadia

GRADE 4, JANUARY

I gave my class a problem involving linear growth, which I wanted them to graph. Prior to this activity, my students had not been exposed to this kind of graphing. I was curious about what they would do.

 At White Mountain School, students are collecting bottles to be exchanged at their local supermarket for money to donate to a hospital in their town. In a fourth-grade class, this is what some of the children brought during the 14 days of the drive.

1. Zelda started out with 30 bottles and brought in 2 bottles every day.

2. Mario started out with 10 bottles and brought in 5 bottles every day.

3. Anna started out with 40 bottles and brought in 1 bottle every day.

4. Ben didn't have any bottles at home to start, but then he brought in 8 bottles every day.

I asked my students to read the information given about the children. Just by reading it, could they tell who was going to be the one to bring in the most bottles? I asked them to do this because I wanted them to see that the information served a greater purpose than for simply filling out charts and creating graphs. My goal was for students to develop an understanding of the data and predict an outcome.

Chloe spoke up first saying that Mario brought in the greatest number of bottles. When she explained, it seemed she was ignoring the initial number of bottles the students had, and she also ignored Ben. Then Wang explained how to calculate the number of bottles for each child. "If we count 15 days," he said, "Zelda had 60; Mario had 85; Anna had 55; and Ben had 120. Because the drive only lasted for 14 days, we have to subtract 1 day for each child so Zelda had 58; Mario had 80; Anna had 54; and Ben had 112."

Students then worked to produce graphs to represent the information. I asked them to do all four graphs on one piece of paper. I had two reasons to impose this constraint: 1) When numbers get too high, students will often tape papers together to reach the largest number. I hoped that by asking them to use one piece of paper, they would be forced to think about how to prepare the graph to fit their data. 2) If they graphed all the data on one page, they would be able to compare graphs. Perhaps they would even overlap the graphs and make some interesting discoveries.

My class had many different ways of organizing their data into graphs. However, as I looked at the variety of graphs, they seemed to fall into several categories.

Quite a few students created graphs showing the final number of bottles each student brought in over the 2 weeks. Carl's graph looked like this:

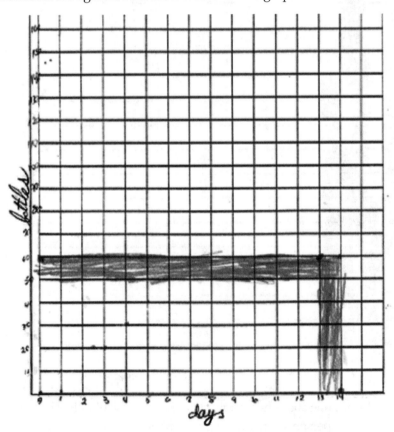

When I asked him about it, he said, "60 bottles here," showing me that the vertical axis counted every 10 bottles, "and 14 days here," pointing to the horizontal axis. This was his graph of the bottles Zelda brought in.

Adrianne also graphed only the final number of bottles. Her page looked like this:

285

290

295

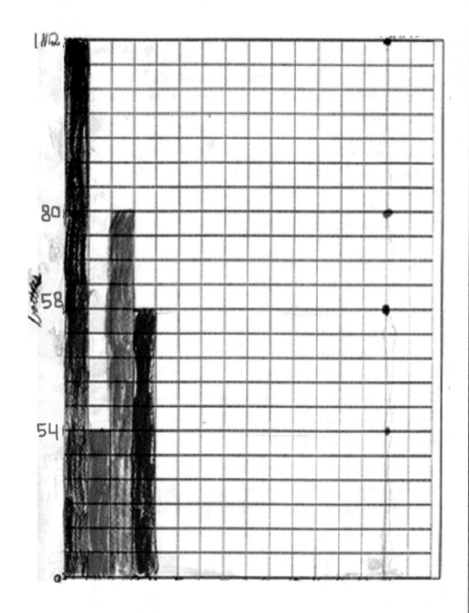

When I asked Adrianne about her graph, she described the details: The number of bottles each person started with, the number each brought in each day, and the total number for the 2 weeks. I said to her, "Adrianne, that's great. You know what? It would be great to have a graph of all the information you just gave me. In your graph, I only see the total after 14 days. How can we create a graph that shows the progression of bottle collection you just described?"

Adrianne said, "I know, you want me to do it again."

Comparing Linear Functions

I said, "Yes, please. You have a very interesting bar graph that shows
what happened at the end. Can you think of how you might make a graph
that shows what's going on all the days before that?"

As I look at Adrianne's graph more closely, I see that equal increments
on the *y*-axis do not represent equal numbers of bottles. That is something
I will still need to work on with her.

Robyn also used a bar graph but included all the data I was asking
Adrianne to show.

305

310

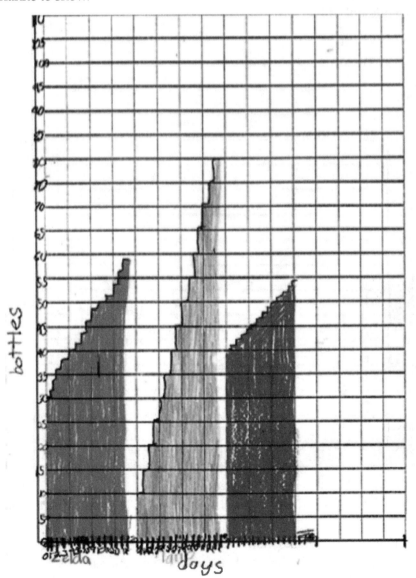

Robyn explained, "On the left side is the number of bottles and on the bottom side is how many days. For Zelda, she had 30 bottles already and then she brought 2 bottles every day. So every day she added 2 more bottles to what she had before. So, on Day 7, for example, she had 44, and on Day, 8 she'll have 2 more, 46. It's the same with the others, except the number of bottles is different." 315

Once Robyn adds the graph for Ben, she will be able to see the information for all four children. 320

Marla's work looked like this:

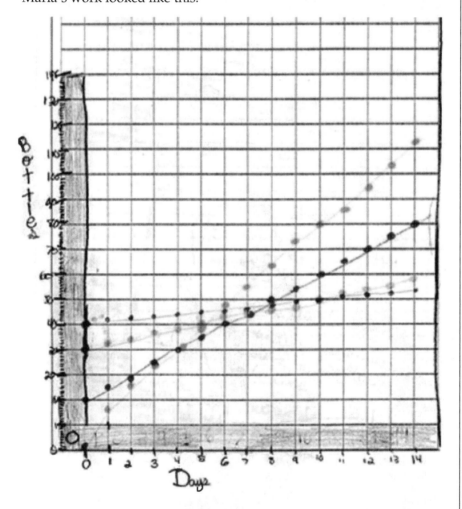

I did not have a chance to talk to Marla, but her graph most closely resembles a conventional representation for graphing functions.

Nadia

For tomorrow's lesson, I am going to recreate these different representations to make them easier for others to read. I will also show only the graphs that represent Zelda's and Anna's bottles, so the students will be comparing just two sets of data. Then I will have a discussion about what we notice. I am curious about whether students will be able to interpret each of their classmates' representations and, especially, what information they can extract from Marla's graphs. Will they be able to tell me, for example, when Zelda and Anna had the same number of bottles? What happened before that and what happened after?

325

330

C H A P T E R

5

Does Doubling Work?

A class of high school students was given a homework problem about polygons arranged in a row. As shown below, a single pentagon with each side equal to 1 unit has a perimeter of 5 units. When 2 such pentagons are joined to share a side, the resulting figure has a perimeter of 8 units. When 3 such pentagons are joined, the resulting figure has a perimeter of 11 units. The assignment was to determine the perimeter of 9 joined pentagons, 100 joined pentagons, and k joined pentagons.

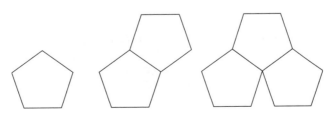

When the teacher, Donna Scanlon, checked her students' homework, she found that most did not solve the problem correctly. However, what was most surprising was that many students had the same wrong answer for the perimeter of 9 joined pentagons: 33 units instead of the correct answer of 29 units. Scanlon wrote, "I was puzzled by this. I was quite sure they wouldn't bother copying someone else's answer unless they could explain it, because that was an often-reinforced classroom expectation. Students knew that they would be asked for explanations. Also, it was not a few students; it was many who had 33 for the answer."

Once the class began to discuss the problem, Nathan offered his thinking. "Well, 3 pentagons have a perimeter of 11. So 9 pentagons should have a perimeter of 3 times that."

His classmate, Lisette, elaborated, "He's saying that 9 is 3 times as big as 3, so the perimeter should be 3 times bigger and 3 times 11 is 33." (Scanlon, 1996, pp. 68–69).

Eventually, students in Scanlon's class correctly solved the problem involving the joined pentagons. However, the lesson here is that students' first impulse was to think that the number of joined pentagons and the perimeter of the figure are proportional: If you double one, you double the other; if you triple one, you triple the other.

There are many situations in which two quantities do form a proportional relationship, and when they do, it is important to notice. Indeed, it is an effective strategy to be able to double (triple, quadruple) one quantity and then double (triple, quadruple) the other.

This chapter presents cases in which students in Grades 1 through 8 are sorting out these ideas. How do proportional relationships help us to predict one quantity from another? How can we tell if a function is, in fact, a proportional relationship?

Scanlon, D. (1996). Algebra is Cool: Reflections on a Changing Pedagogy in an Urban Setting. In D. Schifter (Eds.), *What's Happening in Math Class? Volume 1, Envisioning practices through teacher narratives* (pp. 65–74). New York: Teachers College Press.

5- and 10-floor buildings

Dan

GRADE 2, MARCH

My class was working on an activity about the total number of rooms in buildings with different numbers of floors. For example, they were told that some buildings had 2 rooms on each floor. How many rooms would be in a building with just 1 floor? 2 floors? 3 floors?

We spent some time during our whole-class discussion finding the total number of rooms in a building when each floor had 3 rooms. The activity sheet had asked them to find the number of rooms if the building had 1 floor, 2 floors, 3 floors, 4 floors, 5 floors, and 10 floors. Time was up before we got to all the ideas I wanted to address, and so we continued the next day. Most students had determined the number of rooms on 10 floors by counting or adding. I wanted to give those students who doubled the number of rooms in a 5-floor building to find the number of rooms in a 10-floor building an opportunity to explain their thinking.

TEACHER: Yesterday, we ended our session by discussing your strategies for figuring the total number of rooms if Building A had 10 floors. Not everyone got to share his or her strategies, so I wanted to give you a chance to do so this morning. Sam, you had an interesting way of approaching the problem. Can you tell the class what you did?

SAM: I doubled 15 and got 30.

KAREN: I did, too.

TEACHER: That's right, Karen, you did, too.

At this point, some students seemed to connect with Karen's and Sam's ideas. I heard a few say, "Oh, yeah." This seemed to confirm my suspicion that many just did not see it yesterday. However, there were some who seemed unsure of what Sam was saying.

TEACHER:	Can you explain why you did that? How did you know it would work?	
SAM:	Well, you have 15 and then 5 more is 15 more. So 15 + 15 is 30.	
TEACHER:	I know what you mean, but I'm wondering if you could explain it in more detail. What do you mean, 5 more is 15 more?	30
SAM:	If you have 5 floors, you get 15. So if you go to 10 floors, that's 5 more floors.	
KAREN:	5 + 5 is 10. It's doubling.	
SAM:	Yeah, so you have to double the other side, too. 15 + 15.	35
KAREN:	It's like you're adding the same thing. See. (She takes a 10-floor model and breaks it in half). This is 5 floors (holding one half of the building) and this is 5 more floors (holding the other half).	
TEACHER:	How many rooms are in each?	40
BOTH:	15	
KAREN:	You put them back together and get 30 rooms.	

There were some nods of understanding and some looks of confusion from the other students. I did not want to push this concept so early in the unit, so I moved on. My students will encounter similar problems many times this week and will have plenty of opportunities to work with that idea.

C A S E   **18**

Cookies and candies

Jessica

I gave my class the following problem:

Does Doubling Work?

Jessica

? One day, I made cookie men with my big sister. I used 2 mints for the eyes and 1 mint for the nose on each one. How many mints did I use for 5 cookies?

50

Students started working, some by themselves, some in pairs. Their fingers came out immediately. It was not long before their hands were up with their answers.

Sharon gave an answer of 15. She explained that she used her fingers. She counted each part of her fingers, plus 1 extra because the thumb only has 2 parts. She explained that each finger was a cookie, and each part of the finger was a mint.

55

Nathan had the strategy of counting by 3s: 3, 6, 9, 12, 15. He used his fingers so he would know when he should stop counting. Others counted 3, 6, 9 and then counted up three 1s to 12 and again to 15.

60

I decided this would be a good time to see what students would do if I asked them to go from 5 cookies to 10 cookies. First, I drew a table.

Number of Cookies	Number of Mints
1	3
2	6
3	9
4	12
5	15

I asked the question: "If it took 15 mints to make 5 cookies, then how many mints would I need to make 10 cookies?"

65

Hands went up very quickly. The only problem was the answer most of them had was 18. They had just added 3 mints.

Colleen looked at me and saw from my expression that 18 was not the correct answer. She was not sure why, but she knew I was looking for something else.

70

I restated the problem, this time emphasizing that we had the number of mints needed for *5* cookies and were trying to find the number of mints needed to make *10* cookies. Colleen took a little time, got her fingers working, and shot her hand up in the air. She had the answer of 30: 15 + 15 = 30. She came up to the chart and showed everyone that I had jumped from 5 all the way up to 10.

75

The cookies doubled from 5 to 10, so the mints had to double, again 15 + 15 = 30.

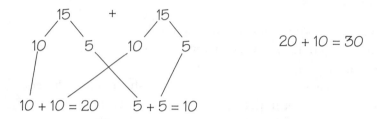

$$20 + 10 = 30$$

I added this information to the table: 10 in the cookies column and 30 in the candies column. Now, since they had listened to Colleen's explanation, I added a 20 under the cookies column of the table, and asked, "How many mints would I need to make 20 cookies?"

Two different answers were given, 45 and 60. Some understood Colleen's explanation and doubled the 30, but others had added the 15 from the 5 cookies and the 30 from the 10 cookies (the last two rows of the table) to get 45.

Billy explained, using the table, that 20 cookies was really 10 + 10, so the mints would be 30 + 30, which equals 60.

The numbers were getting large now, but the class asked if they could find the number of mints needed to make 40 cookies, so I added it to the chart. Billy commented to the class, "Now remember 40 = 20 + 20." Students were working together now—the numbers were large enough that they all needed more hands to figure it out. I thought I had lost quite a few students but let them continue as this was the last of the problems. With time, they figured it out, 60 + 60 = 120.

Tom said, "I looked back at the table, and I saw that 10 cookies had 30 mints. I knew that 40 would be 4 of the 10s. So, I added 30 + 30 = 60, 60 + 30 = 90, and 90 + 30 = 120."

My students have seen tables like this before and they have tried to use them on their own. They were able to see the relationship between the cookies and the mints; each time a cookie was added to the chart, they had to add 3 mints. However, jumping from 5 cookies to 10 cookies was difficult at first.

When I asked them how many mints were needed to make 20 cookies, I got the answer 45. It was the wrong answer, but they were looking at the chart and trying to use it by adding the 15 mints needed for the 5 cookies to the 30 mints needed for the 10 cookies. They later realized that 5 + 10 only gave them 15 cookies, not 20.

Does Doubling Work?

So, had the table helped them or hurt them? Could they have figured the problem out if the table was not there? What information do they need to keep straight in order to solve these kinds of problems?

110

Growing worms, 1

Ruth

I chose a group of five children to try a lesson from the NCTM *Navigations in Algebra* series, "Watch Them Grow." Students were shown a "1-day-old worm," a "2-day-old worm," and a "3-day-old worm" made from isosceles triangles.

My plan was to have the children discuss the pattern and focus on stating the rule for the pattern we were creating with this growing worm. We would record the data on a table and look for the relationship between the age of the worm and the number of triangles used. Up until now, we have focused more on patterns that allow you to double what you know to find a new amount. For example, to find the 10th number in a pattern, students can double the 5th number, or combine the 7th and 3rd number. I wanted them to work on a pattern that does not necessarily allow this to happen. During the lesson, students were involved with such a rich discussion of how the worm was growing, so we only focused on the rule toward the very end.

115

120

After I showed the group the growing worms for the first 3 days, the children were eager to say what they noticed. Manuel immediately said that he knows that 2 halves make a whole; on Day 1, there is 1 whole or 2 halves; on Day 2, there are 2 wholes or 4 halves; and on Day 3, there are 3 wholes or 6 halves. I think that this idea helped the group get started because throughout the lesson they kept referring back to Manuel's halves and wholes, or the

125

triangles and squares. Fatima noticed the squares. She said that Day 1 had 1 square; Day 2 had 2 squares; and Day 3 had 3 squares. She mentioned that the number of squares are growing. Cyndi noticed a pattern of counting by 2s. Day 1 had 2, Day 2 had 4, and Day 3 had 6. It was not until I asked her to clarify what she was naming that she referred to the triangles in the middle of the worm. Interestingly, during the first five minutes of discussion, no one mentioned the 2 constant triangles at the ends of the worm. Each child referred to the middle of the worm, the part that was growing. Is that because they see that the 2 end triangles have not changed? Are they not counting these? I chose not to say anything yet and let them explore their ideas a bit more.

I then asked the class to show what the worm would look like at 4 days old. They all took time to build it, and all were successful. We talked a bit about this.

TEACHER: How did you know how to create the 4-day-old worm?

MANUEL: Well, Day 1 has 1 in the middle, Day 2 has 2 in the middle, so Day 4 has to have 4 in the middle. The middle is going up by 2s.

TEACHER: Can you explain your idea a little more?

MANUEL: See (pointing to our models), this worm has only 1 square, and it is 1 day old. This worm has 2 squares, and it is 2 days old. It keeps going up by 1s in a pattern. So I guess that Day 4 has to have 4 squares.

TEACHER: You also mentioned about the middle going up by 2s. What did you mean by that?

MANUEL: Oh, I was looking at the triangles. It's like what I noticed before, 2 triangles make a whole, so I can count by squares or triangles.

TENEESHA: I get what he is saying. You can count the squares or the triangles. I think I was looking at the triangles. I think that Day 1 has 2 triangles, Day 2 has 4 triangles, Day 3 has 6 triangles, so that means Day 4 has 8 triangles. It's counting by 2s. I could keep going, too.

CYNDI: What about the other triangles?

TEACHER: What triangles are you referring to?

Does Doubling Work?

CYNDI: These on the end. Each worm has to have those. Are they important, too? 165

With Cyndi's mention of the 2 triangles on the ends of each worm, I decided to discuss the total number of triangles used for the worm each day. As a group, we made a table that showed the age of the worm (in days) and the number of triangles used to create the worm. I was wondering if students would include the constant triangles in their count. This is what 170 our table looked like:

Age of Worm (days)	Number of Triangles
1	4
2	6
3	8
4	10
5	
10	

The students all agreed at this time that when counting the number of triangles that made the worm, you had to include the 2 triangles on either end. There was no mention of why we did not discuss them earlier. I asked them to determine how many triangles would be needed to create the 175 worm on the 5th day. Four out of the five children knew the answer immediately; Teneesha needed to build it, so we gave her time. All students said that on Day 5, the worm would be made out of 12 triangles. I was not sure at this time if they were focusing on the relationship between the age of the worm and the number of triangles or if they were just counting by 2s. 180 I decided to continue with this exploration and see how they would figure out the number of triangles needed on Day 10.

Immediately, two of the children created a table. One began where we left off on Day 5, and the other began with Day 1. They both got the correct answer,

22, for Day 10, but did they see a relationship? I decided to begin discussing the methods used by students who got 20 and 24 triangles for their answers.

Manuel was first. He wrote, "20 because it is counting by 2s, but it just started at 4, not 2. $10 \times 2 = 20$."

TEACHER: Let's talk about Manuel's answer, he got 20 triangles. What did he do?

TENEESHA: He counted by 2s with multiplication.

CYNDI: I'm not sure if I agree with his final answer, but what he did does make sense. He counted by 2s, I think, because we add 2 more triangles to the worm each day.

TEACHER: I'm wondering why Manuel said that it counts by 2s, but it started at 4.

MANUEL: I said that because our chart begins with 4 triangles for the worm on Day 1. But, then it does go up by 2s.

TEACHER: (I decide that I will return to Manuel's explanation later.) Let's look at Cyndi's and Harvey's strategy. Both of them added 12 + 12. Can we talk about that?

HARVEY: I added two 12s because I doubled. If you have Day 5, and it is 12 triangles, then double the 12, and you get to Day 10, which is the double of Day 5.

CYNDI: I did the same thing, but I used multiplication. I think we can do that because we know how to double. But when I checked my strategy with the table, I came up with a different answer. I think the table is right, but I'm not sure why. I thought about 10 triangles in the middle and then 2 on the end, so that's 12. I doubled the 10 and the 2 and got 24 triangles.

TEACHER: Teneesha has the worm at 5 days old in front of her; let's look at that. According to Harvey and Cyndi, we should double this to get to Day 10, let's do that.

Teneesha made the other Day-5 worm and put it next to the original.

Ruth

I kept the shapes displayed for a few minutes while the students looked at them. Teneesha was the first to speak and pointed out that our model really looks like 2 worms. She said that it has 2 heads and 2 tails. What a great way to think about this! She continued to say that you are supposed to have only 10 squares in the middle because it is 10 days old, plus the head and tail on the end. I was impressed with her thinking because I had not been sure if she completely understood what the other students had been talking about. She was the one student in the group who needed to build the worms to verify the number of triangles, and she also started her table from Day 1 and seemed to just count by 2s. I did not think that she was noticing the relationship between the age of the worm and the number of triangles used, but evidently seeing it built was helping her make that connection.

From this, Manuel pointed out that we needed to remove the extra head and tail because we can count those only once. He stated that a worm should have only 1 head and 1 tail, and that left 22 triangles. I asked him again about his response earlier, and he said that he figured out why he got 20 triangles. He made the connection with the table starting at 4 because 2 triangles were in the middle and the other 2 were the head and tail. He decided that he counted only the triangles on the body, leaving out the head and tail.

At this point, we started to generalize our rule. I asked how we could use the discoveries we had made to figure out the number of triangles for a worm 15 days old, 20 days old, and 100 days old.

CYNDI: I think that I notice something. We know that we have to keep adding the triangles on the end, so that's just like adding 2 more each time. When we did the 10-day-old worm, the body was double the number of days. Like, 10 days is the same as 20 triangles.

FATIMA: Yeah, the number of squares in the middle is the same as the day of the worm. And, then we have to double that because we want to know triangles and Manuel said that 2 halves make a whole.

CYNDI: Don't forget "plus 2."

TEACHER: I'm wondering how we can use this to figure out the number of triangles for any age of the worm. How about a 20-day-old worm?

CYNDI:	So 20 days would be 20 squares, so double that for the triangles—40. Then we do 40 + 2 = 42 triangles.
TEACHER:	How about a worm 100 days old?
MANUEL:	202
TEACHER:	How did you get that so quickly?
MANUEL:	It's 200 because that's how many triangles would be in the body. That's 100 doubled. I got 2 because of the head and tail.
TEACHER:	Can anyone make a rule so we could find out the number of triangles for any age of the worm? Think about what we have just talked about.
FATIMA:	I think I have an idea. We just say the age and then times it by 2, that gets us the body triangles. Then we add 2 more for the head and tail.

I wrote this idea on the board: (age of the worm × 2) + 2. We tried our rule for other ages of the worm, such as 25 and 40, numbers the students felt comfortable doubling. We kept referring to the rule and why it works after we solved each one. I was impressed with their thinking. We did not get as far along as I had thought (my original plan was to focus more on the rule, allowing them to then create their own growing pattern and formulate a new rule), but we got a lot accomplished. Perhaps I will work with them another time to see if they can generalize a rule for a different growing pattern and use it to find the rule for the nth number of that pattern. By the end of this lesson, all of these students were able to describe the growing pattern in their own words and explain what was happening and why we needed to keep the 2 extra triangles on the end. I think Teneesha struggled a bit, but in the end she helped the other students to remember those 2 additional triangles by naming them the "head" and "tail" of the worm.

Growing worms, 2

James

GRADE 5, APRIL

I presented my students with the task called "Watch Them Grow" from
NCTM's *Navigations in Algebra*. In this activity, students explore the growth
of a "worm" made from isosceles right triangles. During previous months,
we had worked on creating, building, extending, and describing patterns
at varying levels of success. I figured this was the perfect opportunity to
revisit these ideas and see in what ways, if any, my students' thinking may
have developed.

285

I introduced the activity to my students and showed them what a
1-day-old worm looked like.

290

I took some suggestions from the class as to how they thought the
worm might grow into a 2-day-old worm. Students presented a variety of growth patterns, and I told them those were all possibilities.
Today there was one growth pattern we would pursue: Each day, 2
more isosceles right triangles would be added in the middle between
the 2 end triangles. I distributed plastic triangles, and they were able
to extend this pattern as I asked them to build a 3-day-old worm by
placing more isosceles right triangles between the end triangles to get
a pattern like this:

295

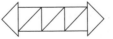

I then asked students to take out 8 more isosceles right triangle pieces.
I assigned them the task of trying to figure out how many triangles it
would take to construct a worm that was 20 days old. Some students were
complaining about there not being enough triangles to make a 20-day-old
worm, while others began building worms and writing down information

300

about each worm they built. I gave each pair of students about 10 minutes to work on some of the ideas they had before I brought the discussion back to the entire class.

TEACHER: How did people do, figuring out how many triangles are in a 20-day-old worm?

There were mixed responses from the class—different answers and calls of "It was hard" and the like.

TEACHER: What made this task difficult for some of you?

DANEISHA: There weren't enough triangles to make a 20-day-old worm. We didn't know what to do to try to figure it out ...

TEACHER: Was there anyone in the class that was able to figure out a way to get past the lack of triangles?

JANELLE: Well, I made the first few worms and counted how many were in those. I noticed there were 12 triangles in the 5-day-old worm. I know that 5 is $\frac{1}{4}$ of 20, so I multiplied 12 times 4 and got 48. I think there are 48 triangles in the 20-day-old worm.

TEACHER: You have an interesting strategy to consider. Does your idea work when you use other ages of the worm? For example, could I use the same strategy for a 4-day-old worm?

JANELLE: You should be able to.

TEACHER: Try it ...

JANELLE: Well, 1 is $\frac{1}{4}$ of 4. So, if I multiply 4 times 4, a 4-day-old worm should have 16 triangles. Wait ...

TEACHER: What's the problem?

JANELLE: When I made the 4-day-old worm, it only had 10 triangles.

TEACHER: Hmm, so your idea doesn't seem to work. I wonder why not. Are there other ideas?

At this point, the bell rang and it was time for lunch. We decided we would pick up where we left off after we ate. After lunch, we reconvened.

TEACHER: Before we get back to where we were, I want to ask the class something. How are people keeping track of their information about the worms?

A few ideas came out ... "I drew pictures," "I wrote it down," "I kept it in a chart." I pursued the chart response.

TEACHER:	I heard some people say they made a chart. Can you show me how you made it?

340

Kevin approached the board.

KEVIN:	I used 2 columns—one was for the days old the worm was. The second one was for how many triangles it was when it was that old.

Together, the class filled in Kevin's chart up to the 5-day-old worm.

345

TEACHER:	We'll be able to use this chart as we talk more about our patterns. OK, so did anyone have any other ideas about how to figure out how many triangles are in a 20-day-old worm?

JANELLE:	Well, I thought some more about it at lunch and came up with another idea ... I saw that there were 4 triangles in a 1-day-old worm. So, I added 4 up 20 times to get how many would be in a 20-day-old worm. Now I think there will be 80 triangles in it.

350

TEACHER:	Another helpful idea, Janelle. What do people think about this?

MARCUS:	I don't think it's totally right. When I look at the chart, I only see the worm getting bigger by 2 triangles every time. In Janelle's way it gets bigger by 4 each time. I think 80 is too many.

355

TEACHER:	So do you have any suggestions?

MARCUS:	I think that maybe you could cut 80 in half and that might get you the answer. Since it only grows by 2 every time instead of 4, 2 is half of 4. I think there will be 40 triangles in a 20-day-old worm.

360

FARIQ:	I think Marcus is right, but we don't start at 2, we start at 4 ... I think the answer will be different.

365

TEACHER:	What do you mean?

FARIQ:	I can't really explain it ... I just know that we don't start at 2. If we started at 2 it would be 40, but we start at 4.

KEITH: I get what she's saying ... Look at the worm. In the first day it has the 2 middle triangles that make the square ... that's how much each worm grows every day. But, on the first day you also have to add the end triangles. That's what makes it 4 at the start.   370

TEACHER: Wow, that's really neat. Good explaining Keith. So let's take a look at what we just came up with. We started out with Janelle's idea that it was 4 triangles for each day, so 20 days would get us 80 triangles. How did Janelle get that answer?   375

CLASS: 20 × 4!

TEACHER: OK, good. What does the 20 stand for in this expression?

CLASS: The number of days old the worm is.   380

TEACHER: Good ... can anyone help me out and tell me—is there a way that I could talk about Janelle's idea for any number of days old the worm is?

This began a conversation about variables and what we could do if we wanted to use something to represent *any* number. As a class we came to   385
the conclusion that we would use the letter a to stand for the age of the worm. We agreed that Janelle was saying that the number of triangles in a worm would be 4 times the number of days old it was, or 4 times a, or $4a$.

TEACHER: So, what did Marcus say we should do with Janelle's idea?

CLASS: Cut it in half.   390

TEACHER: So, using what we figured out with Janelle's idea, how could we say that?

CLASS: $4a$ divided by 2.

MARCUS: Or $2a$, since 2 is half of 4.

TEACHER: Very good, Marcus. OK, so does that get us the correct   395
number of triangles for any age of the worm? How could we tell?

OFER: We can compare it to the chart. If the worm is 2 days old, then it should have 6 triangles. If we use what we just came up with, then a 2-day-old worm will only have 4 triangles.   400

KAREN: That's because we have to add the 2 end triangles.

FARIQ: Yeah. We should do $2a + 2$.

TEACHER: Will that work for any age, $2a + 2$?

The class plugged in the different ages and found that each answer
we got when using this expression matched the information on our chart. They were satisfied with their work. Using what they figured out, they came to the conclusion that there were 42 triangles in a 20-day old worm. **405**

JANELLE: Mr. Jackson, I see another pattern. I noticed that the number of triangles in a worm is equal to 2 times the next one down on the chart. **410**

TEACHER: Wow! Look at that. What is another way to say what Janelle is telling us? Can anyone give it to me as an expression like we just came up with? Does it work?

OFER: Well, since we are going down the chart, it's like we're adding 1 to the age of the worm. **415**

TEACHER: Good. Does anyone know how we could write this as an expression?

ANDREA: I think it would be $a + 1$.

TEACHER: Good.

OFER: Oh! And since we have to double it, it would be $a + 1$ times 2. **420**

TEACHER: Good.

I wrote on the board the expression $2(a + 1)$, and we had a short discussion about why the expression would appear that way. We then checked to see if it was correct by plugging in numbers and comparing them to the numbers in our chart. The class was thrilled that they were able to find a second way to talk about the pattern. **425**

I thought this was a very good class session as the students were able to work through several stages in their thinking and ultimately come up with two written expressions to describe the "rule" of the growing pattern. I was quite surprised by the ability of students to look at an idea that was incorrect and change it into something that made more sense to them. Also, their ability to take ideas from several individuals and piece them into a general rule made me realize that the students were truly invested in each other's thinking. **430**

The follow-up activity to this lesson was for students to build their own patterns and discover a rule for how their patterns grew. I knew the students would be able to develop patterns, but I was curious to see how they would keep track of their growing patterns and whether they would be able to develop expressions for their rules. Almost every student developed a chart to track his or her data, and almost every student was able to develop an expression for his or her rule. Some students explained their rule in words as opposed to using variables in an algebraic expression. I was definitely both surprised and pleased by this, as these ideas were difficult for students to grasp when they originally encountered this work.

I was also concerned during class that because relatively few students were speaking up as they generated ideas, it was possible that some students were lost or not paying attention to what was going on. I was reassured with this post activity because students were able to incorporate what we had been working on as a group into their own ideas.

C A S E   **21**

What's the formula for square borders? revisited

Nancy

GRADES 7 AND 8, OCTOBER

I gave my students a problem about this sequence of square-border arrangements of tiles. In each figure, the number of tiles in a side is one more than in the previous figure.

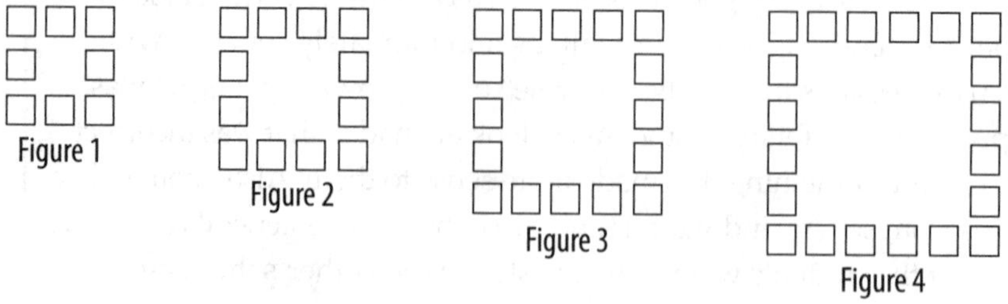

Figure 1

Figure 2

Figure 3

Figure 4

Their task was as follows:

1. Draw Figure 5.

2. Determine how many tiles would be needed for Figure 7.

3. Make a table showing the relationship between each figure number and the number of tiles for the first 10 figures.

4. Find the relationship between the figure number and the number of tiles used.

In Case 11, I described one group of students' work on the problem, including the challenges they faced to find the number of cubes in the 50th figure. When I worked with another group of students, I was interested to see the kinds of errors they made before they, too, could correctly answer the question about Figure 50.

Kevin took this approach: "If Figure 10 had 44 tiles, then add 44 more tiles for a total of 88 to get the number of tiles in Figure 20. Adding another 44 to 88 will equal 132 tiles for Figure 30." Continuing this pattern, he determined that Figure 40 would have 176 tiles, so Figure 50 would have 220 tiles. He assumed that if you just kept adding 44 tiles it would get you to the next 10th figure. I have seen many students do this: find what they think is a pattern and assume it will lead them to the correct answer.

Another student took a similar approach but was a bit more careful in looking for patterns in the table. Benito continued the table to Figure 20 and noticed the following: The difference between Figures 5 and 10 is 20 tiles. So, as you increase the figure number by 5, the number of tiles increases by 20. He determined that Figure 5 has 24 tiles, Figure 10 has 44 tiles, Figure 15 has 64 tiles, Figure 20 has 84 tiles, and Figure 25 has 104 tiles. Then he doubled the number of tiles in Figure 25 (104 + 104 = 208) because he felt that the number of tiles in Figure 50 would be twice the number of tiles in Figure 25. If he had kept going up by 20 tiles for Figures 30, 35, 40, 45, and 50, he would have calculated 204. But doubling it was quicker, and he did not think it would change the pattern he had found.

Sheila and Fran worked hard at constructing the patterns using tiles. This gave them a clearer picture of what was happening as the figure grew. Sheila could see that when adding the tiles together for any figure, such as Figure 8, you add the 2 sides together (10 + 10) and then you add the other 2 sides together not counting the corners (8 + 8) for the total of the number of tiles (20 + 16 = 36). Fran came to the same conclusion but solved it like this: Multiply by 4 the number of tiles in a side (4 × 10); then subtract the tiles that are counted twice, the ones on the corners (40 − 4 = 36).

490

When Sheila and Fran were attempting to find the number of tiles in the 50th figure, the challenge was to determine the number of tiles on a side. At first, Sheila did what other students had done and said that there were 50 tiles on the side of the 50th figure. She added 50 + 50 + 50 + 50 = 200; then she subtracted 4 tiles to get a total of 196 tiles. I questioned her about the number of tiles, and she realized that Figure 50 would have 52 tiles on its side, noticing the pattern that the number of tiles on a side of the figure is 2 greater than the figure number. She then calculated 52 + 52 + 52 + 52 = 208; 208 − 4 tiles = 204 tiles total.

495

Fran and Sheila's work was the clearest for holding onto the meaning of the numbers involved in the pattern they discovered. Actually creating the model seems to help them see the pattern with clearer understanding.

500

C A S E   **22**

Penny Jar revisited

GRADE 4, MAY

My students were working on a Penny Jar problem:

> The penny jar started with 2 pennies in it. Each round, 5 more pennies were added.

505

Students found how many pennies were in the jar after 1, 2, 3, 4, 5, 10, and 15 rounds. I had expected someone to double the number of pennies for Round 5 to find the number of pennies for Round 10, but I had not expected anyone who used that strategy to make it work correctly!

510

However, Lynn explained that, in order to solve for Round 10, she doubled the number of pennies in Round 5 (2 × 27 = 54) and then subtracted the start number (54 − 2 = 52). She said, "The 27 pennies

Does Doubling Work?

from Round 5 already includes the start number. When you double it, you have 2 start numbers in your total, and so you have to take one out."

515

Karl took this idea further, pointing out that you could triple the number of pennies in Round 5 to find the number of pennies in Round 15 ($3 \times 27 = 81$), but then you have to remember to remove the 2 extra start numbers ($81 - 4 = 77$).

C H A P T E R

6

Examining Non-Constant Rate of Change

Consider the following Penny Jar situation. Start with 0 pennies in the jar. In Round 1, put 1 penny in the jar; in Round 2, put in 2 pennies for a total of 3 pennies in the jar; in Round 3, put in 3 pennies for a total of 6 pennies, and so on. A table representing this situation would be:

Number of Rounds	Number of Pennies in the Jar
0	0
1	1
2	3
3	6
4	10

As the number of rounds increases by 1, the number of pennies in the jar increases, but not by a constant amount. This is different from a linear function in which, as one variable changes at a constant rate, so does the other. For example, in Henrietta's roost, which describes a linear function, every time Henrietta's position changes by 1, the number of hens sitting in the row changes by 2.

In this chapter, students explore nonlinear functions: as one quantity changes by a constant rate, the other does not. However, as students discover, with these particular functions, the second quantity does change in a regular way. As you read the cases, pay attention to the pattern that defines the way the second quantity changes. Can you find a formula that relates one quantity to the other?

C A S E   **23**

Fastwalker

Lucy
GRADE 3, MAY

My class has been working with graphs throughout the year. Each Wednesday, we have plotted the morning temperature in our small town. Students also interpreted and plotted graphs to determine how the temperature rose and fell over the course of a day, a month, and a year in various places around the world. Then they worked on a set of activities involving a scenario in which children accumulated allowances of marbles at different rates. As part of this work, they graphed and compared different rates of change. For about a week, the class has been looking at how imaginary animals grow on a fantasy planet. In both the marble and animal growth graphs, the rates of change are constant. For example, a child might receive 3 marbles each night or an animal might grow 3 centimeters each year.

During the work about accumulating marbles, students were really paying attention to the slope of the graphs. They noticed the steepness of the diagonal lines and could describe the different rates of change. When comparing two different rates on the same graph, they could explain why

5

10

15

Examining Non-Constant Rate of Change

the lines intersected at a certain place. They described steady but faster rates because one character received 2 more marbles each day or grew 2 centimeters more than the other each year. They understood that even if one started out with more marbles or was taller, if the other character received enough more each day or year than the first, he or she would catch | 20
up and pull ahead of the other. It was like a race, my students explained: "Like the runner who is always running faster." My students could also explain why one child or animal would never catch up to the other.

For each of these scenarios, the graphs were straight lines because the rate of change was constant. However, at the end of the unit, the children | 25
met a new animal that grew differently from the others they had looked at. Here is the table that shows how Fastwalker grew over a number of years.

Age (years)	Height (centimeters)
0 (birth)	1
1	2
2	4
3	7
4	11
5	16
6	22

As soon as the children saw the numbers on the table, they knew this situation was going to be different than others that they had studied. "It does not grow steady," Ethan explained. Moira said, "It grows different | 30
each year than other animals." It only took a few minutes for them to figure out the number pattern.

They had figured out that there was an increase of 1 over the growth from the previous year. After completing the table for the growth of Fastwalker up to the age of 12, students made several observations. | 35

■ Each year Fastwalker grows more the age it is becoming.
■ Fastwalker grows 1 more centimeter than the last amount each year starting at 1.
■ The 1 is plussing from the previous year (age).

- The 1 is the 1 centimeter that it was at birth.
- It grows at a switchable rate.

After students filled in the table and felt satisfied that they understood what was happening, I asked what they thought the graph would look like. John said it would be like the edge of a circle. He used his hand to draw in the air a curved line that sloped up. Brad said it would get steep. Geoff said that it would start out not steep and then get steeper really fast. He took his hand and made a gentle slope at first then curved it and shot his hand up over his head. There were many sounds of agreement from the rest of the class.

The children then plotted their graphs and were really excited by how different it looked from any of the other graphs they had done. Sally wrote that the graph looked like half of a tree trunk. Harry wrote that it looked like the outside of a circle.

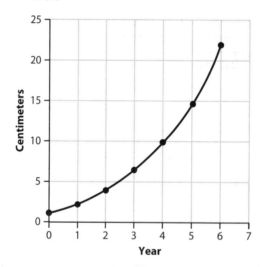

As we started the discussion, there were hands popping up all over the room. Students were very interested in this graph that looked so different from the ones we had worked with before.

JACK: It changes.

TEACHER: What do you mean?

JACK: It's not steady because it doesn't go up by the same amount each time.

BRAD: That's why it's [the graph] curved like that.

LINDA: It looks like a wave; it curves, first lightly.

JOSH: It looks like a quarter of a circle.

TEACHER: Why does it look like this?

GEOFF: Because when it goes further, it gets more straight up. The higher the number, the more it goes up. It's going up more than it's going sideways.

65

JACK: The numbers are changing. It's not straight because it doesn't grow at a steady rate.

SANDY: Each time we're adding bigger numbers. It's small at the beginning. But then it's spread out because the numbers are bigger. There's more distance between points [on the graph].

70

JOSH: The higher the number, the more it goes up.

At this point, math class was drawing to a close, but we were all feeling like we had accomplished something important.

C A S E   24

Folding paper

Veronica

GRADE 3, NOVEMBER

My third graders were using a new textbook for the first time, and I wanted to show them the procedure for reading the book and working out the problems on a separate sheet of paper. I gave each child a piece of plain paper and began to show them how to fold the paper so that it was separated into a number of parts—boxes they could number and use for each corresponding problem in the book.

75

80

"Fold your paper in half like this," I said, demonstrating in front of the class. "How many parts does your paper have?"

"2," came a chorus of dutiful students.

"Now fold your paper in half again," I intoned, knowing that this routine of dividing the paper would soon become automatic for them.

85

"How many parts does your paper have now?"

They unfolded their potential answer sheets and responded, "4."

I decided to put some of this information on the board to make it easier for all students to understand. I wrote:

Number of Folds	Number of Parts
1	2
2	4

Seeing what looked like a table, I quickly decided to capitalize on my students' interest and skill in finding patterns. It would be a brief detour to our goal of working on the textbook problems.

"How many parts do you predict we'll have after folding the paper 3 times?"

"6," was the confident reply of many voices. So, we folded, unfolded, and counted. "8!" ("How did that happen?" was written on their faces.)

"What is happening?" I asked.

While many children were still pondering both the surprise and my question, Nikki volunteered, "Every time you fold, you cut each part into 2 parts."

A few of the students had light bulbs go off, so I persevered, first adding to the table and then asking the inevitable, "If you folded the paper 4 times, how many parts would there be?"

Number of Folds	Number of Parts
1	2
2	4
3	8
4	?

Their guesses ranged from 10 to 12 to 16.

However, this time a few more students seemed to understand that with every fold, each part was halved, and therefore, there were twice as many sections. Some children noticed the doubling pattern in the table.

I tried to connect both ideas by making a diagram on the board that showed each box being halved, but I was not sure how much students understood. So, while drawing and explaining orally, I thought to myself about what to do next. Do I assume that everyone gained some knowledge of the pattern and proceed with the instructions for working on the math book pages? Or, do we continue exploring the pattern so everyone could catch on?

Without consciously deciding, this challenge came out of my mouth, "Figure out how many parts or boxes there would be on the paper if we folded it 8 times." My cooperative, enthusiastic group quickly gathered scrap paper and pencils and most of them began working on the task. Our math hour, designated for practicing another skill, was dwindling. However, the children were involved in an interesting problem that required logical thinking and computation practice.

Here are a few examples of how the problem was solved:

Chris attempted to fold his paper 8 times, found it too difficult and stopped at 5—counting the boxes folded into his paper for a total of 32. When reminded that we were looking for an answer to 8 folds, he said, "I have to do it 3 more times." So he added 3 more sets of 8—32 + 8 + 8 + 8—and got a total of 56. Confusing 8 folds with adding groups of 8 kept Chris's answer very low. However, no one yet suspected that the correct answer would be 256!

Lauren could not see any pattern at first, "It's plussing. No, it's timesing. No, it's plussing until 3 ... 1 + 1 = 2, 2 + 2 = 4, 3 + 3 ..."

I was confused, too, until I realized she was reading the table left to right. When we went back to actually folding the paper, she was able to explain the table, "You add 4 twice, you get 8. You add 8 twice, you get 16." Then she was on her way to the big number.

Peter got a total of 64 by making a grid on his paper that was 8 spaces by 8 spaces. His method seemed so logical I could not think how to steer him in the right direction. So, I waited for others to show their strategies and hoped Peter would "catch on."

Luckily, many students were able to see the pattern and continued the table by doubling each previous total. At first, the children thought their answer of 256 must be wrong because it was so large. However, they re-checked their math and talked with their tablemates to confirm the number. It was fun to see their amazement at how quickly the total grew.

I felt so excited that I had spontaneously allowed an activity to happen that built on and extended our work with patterns, that fit a relevant need (to fold paper?), and that allowed the students to compute in their own ways. Other math concepts inadvertently came out of this experience also—discussion of why the answer could not be an odd number, introduction of tables as ways of collecting and using data, and addition strategies, all of which I will follow up with in other contexts.

Yes, we did the textbook pages the next day, and yes every student
folded his or her paper correctly.

C A S E   25

How many outfits?

Jessica

GRADE 1, JUNE

This lesson was an outgrowth of a problem of the day. The children needed
to find clothing combinations. They were told they had 3 shirts: red, blue,
and green; and 3 pairs of pants: red, blue, and green. They needed to find all
of the possible combinations of shirts and pants.

155

The children used many strategies. Some drew the clothes, then cut
them out and moved them around, then recorded. Some used cubes, and
some used lines for matching. There were 9 combinations:

b/b	r/r	g/g
b/r	r/g	g/b
b/g	r/b	g/r

160

Nick's method of solving the problem was to draw squares.

Shirts

Pants

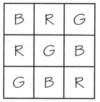

Examining Non-Constant Rate of Change

Jessica

GRADE 1, JUNE

It seemed so clear to Nick, but when he tried to explain his strategy to his classmates, it did take time for some of the students to understand what he was talking about. He did not give up explaining until they all understood his representation. I think it was hard because what he labeled as pants was actually a way to see the outfits.

I collected his work and spent some time reflecting on the class discussion. What would they do if I asked them to find the number of possible combinations with more colors of clothes? Would they be able to see the changes when adding more color choices? I created 7 different worksheets. For the first one, there was only 1 shirt and 1 pair of pants; both were blue. The second had a choice of 2 colors: blue or red shirt and blue or red pants. The third had a choice of 3 colors: blue, red, and green. I continued creating the worksheets, adding one more color each time: yellow, then orange, then purple, and then brown. Students worked in pairs or groups of 3 to come up with all of the possible combinations.

It was interesting to watch the groups. Many tried to use Nick's strategy but just colored in the squares randomly, making sure each color of pants was matched with each color of shirt. However, Charlotte found a more systematic method. This is how her group filled in the worksheet for 7 colors:

Shirts

Bl	R	G	Y	O	P	Br

Pants

Bl	R	G	Y	O	P	Br
Br	Br	Br	Br	Br	Br	P
P	P	P	P	P	O	O
O	O	O	O	Y	Y	Y
Y	Y	Y	G	G	G	G
G	G	R	R	R	R	R
R	Bl	Bl	Bl	Bl	Bl	Bl

When I look at what Charlotte's group wrote, it seems they first created all the solid-color outfits (shirt and pants the same color). Then they created all the mixed-color outfits with brown pants, then with purple pants, then with orange pants, and so on.

After my class finished all the worksheets, I pasted them on a large chart, in order. We used this chart to look for the information that I had asked for—how many combinations are possible for different numbers of colors? In order to organize the information, we made a table.

Number of Colors	Number of Combinations
1	1
2	4
3	9
4	16
5	25
6	36
7	49

Now with the table in front of them, I asked them if there was anything they noticed.

Troy said, "When we had 2, we had two 2s. When we had 3, we had three 3s. When we had 4, we had four 4s."

Elliot jumped up off his rug square at this point all excited, "That's the same as 3×3 and 4×4, that's multiplying."

Nicholas let us know that he knew some multiplication facts, "$2 \times 2 = 4$ and $3 \times 3 = 9$ and $4 \times 4 = 16$ and $5 \times 5 = 25$." He was not sure about 6×6 and 7×7.

I wanted to emphasize how the number combinations were changing, so I brought their attention to the table. I asked if they saw any patterns.

Ben noticed that the number of colors was getting larger by 1. The numbers of combinations were also getting bigger, "From 1 color to 2 colors, it got bigger by 3. From 2 to 3, it got bigger by 5."

I recorded Ben's observations on the table. The class helped fill in the rest of the changes.

185

190

195

200

205

Examining Non-Constant Rate of Change

Number of Colors	Number of Combinations
1	1
	3
2	4
	5
3	9
	7
4	16
	9
5	25
	11
6	36
	13
7	49

Charlotte asked how many combinations there would be if we had 8 colors.

Elliot said, "It's going to be bigger than 7 by 15."

Fingers started flying, and it was not long before 49 + 15 = 64 was announced.

I asked Elliot how he knew it would be bigger by 15. He said, "I noticed that there was a pattern with the 3, 5, 7, 9, 11, 13. Each one got bigger by 2. So if you add 2 to 13, it's 15. The next one would be 15 bigger."

I added this information to the chart.

Number of Colors	Number of Combinations
1	1
	3 → 2
2	4
	5 → 2
3	9
	7 → 2
4	16
	9 → 2
5	25
	11 → 2
6	36
	13 → 2
7	49
	15
8	64

I thought I might really be pushing my luck with their attention span, but because at least half the class was still invested, I asked one more question. "Can you show me, using the grids you made, where the extra ones are, the amount we add on?" They were not sure what I meant, so we went back and looked at all of the combinations. | 220

I said, "OK, let's start back at the beginning—with 1 color, we had 1 combination." I outlined the blue square in black. "Now let's look at 2 colors. You said it got bigger by 3. Where is the 3?"

My students were bouncing now (at least 9 of them were), and they wanted to show me where the extras were. They could see how each | 225 square fit into the next, leaving one column and one row. So, they could see where the 3, 5, 7, 9, 11, 13 were coming from!

At this point the noise in the hall alerted us that it was time for lunch. Thank goodness because I was exhausted!

I am extremely pleased with the progress my students have made dur- | 230 ing this year. They truly have become very focused at looking for patterns and number relationships. I have exposed them to activities that I would never have used in previous years because of the difficulty. They may not understand all of the math involved, but they are looking at new strategies to help their understanding. They were able to see the changes from one | 235 set of colors to the next in both the tables and the corresponding diagrams of squares.

C A S E   26

Playing with squares

One day, my students were making squares by fitting together colored square tiles and began making some discoveries about square numbers. They made many observations about the patterns in which the square | 240

Examining Non-Constant Rate of Change

numbers got bigger and how many tiles were added to an existing square to make the next size square.

They built what we called *growing squares*. They learned that a 2-by-2 square needed 4 tiles, a 3-by-3 needed 9, and so on.

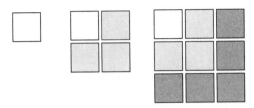

After they built many squares, they made a table with the values they had found.

Size of One Side	Number of Tiles
1	1
2	4
3	9
4	16
5	25
6	36
7	49
8	64
9	81
10	100

I asked them to look at the tiles and also the table to state some observations. It was an impressive list we ended up with as a class:

- 1, 4, and 9 are square numbers.
- 16, 25, 36, 49, 64, 81, and 100 are square numbers.
- Square numbers go odd, even, odd, even....
- If you times a square number by a square number, you get a square number.
- Take any square number, add two 0s to it, and you will get another square number.

- When you add a row at the bottom and a row to the side and make a corner, you get another square number.

I decided to ask the class to work with a partner or in a small group to explore what happens if they start with one square (1 tile) in the center and add more tiles around it.

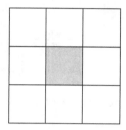

Nuen immediately said, "It will still be a square." This surprised me because of the quickness of her response and the tone of her voice, which conveyed that she was very sure of it. Nuen is a first grader. What did Nuen see right away when she said "It will still be a square"?

All the children got busy in their groups, building squares outside of squares, using a different color for each set of tiles around each square. At first, I noticed that the children were counting the number of tiles they added to make the next bigger square. I wondered whether they were only looking at the border of the square, which is the new color of tiles they used. I asked Basha to show me her square.

BASHA: This is my new square (pointing her finger around the square). I count all the squares I just added around the smaller square, but I included all the other squares inside it.

NUEN: There are squares inside squares. First a 1-by-1, then 3-by-3, 5-by-5, 7-by-7, 9-by-9. They are all odds. You skip all the even numbers.

Nuen saw the pattern of how the squares grew. When I asked her to predict what the next square would be, she felt very confident that it would be an 11 by 11. I asked her to build the next square to check her prediction.

After some time, the class gathered in our meeting area to share discoveries:

MELODIE: When you make this square starting with 1 square in the middle, you skip all the even numbers. This is an odd square. Each square has an odd number of tiles.

260

265

270

275

280

Examining Non-Constant Rate of Change

RICK:	You add an equal number of tiles on each side of the square. Each time you add a line around, you include all the squares inside it.		285
KEN:	The number of tiles on each side of the square is always odd. The number of tiles added to each smaller square is always even.		290
LILLIAN:	We couldn't make a 2-by-2 square when we start with one square in the middle. You go 1 by 1, 3 by 3, 5 by 5.		
NANCY:	When you count the number of tiles across, down, or diagonally, the number is always the same.		
PAUL:	The number of tiles in each square is always *odd,* but you add an *even* number of tiles to the previous square. The number of squares you add increases by a multiple of 8. Start with 1 tile; add 8 tiles to make a bigger square, then add 16 tiles to make the next square, then add 24 tiles for the next square.		295

300 |

As Paul was talking I started to make a table like this:

Size of a Square	Number of Tiles	Number of Tiles Added to Make the Next Size Square
1 by 1	1	+8
3 by 3	9	+16
5 by 5	25	+24
7 by 7	49	
9 by 9		
11 by 11		

I stopped at this point and asked them to predict what numbers would complete the table. They did the work, and then they checked with the recordings they had made on their 1-inch grid paper where they colored each square using the same colors as the tiles they had used. This is where we will begin tomorrow.

305

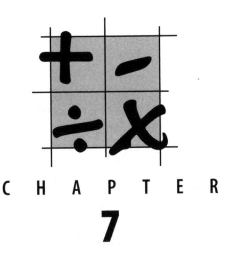

data-based graphs *dep/indep variables (trends) rates of change (area) intervals coordinate grids interpretation*

7

Functions Without Formulas

U p to this point, all the functions that have appeared in the Casebook can be represented as formulas that define how one variable is related to the other. For all of these functions, the output variable changes in a regular way. For example, in a linear function, a constant difference in one variable results in a constant difference in the other. In a quadratic function, the difference of the output variable at each step increases by a fixed amount. In an exponential function, the difference is related to the values of the function (i.e., when the values double, so do the differences), and multiplying by a constant gets you from one value to the next.

There is another kind of function that is not defined by a formula. For example, at a given place on a given day, there is a correspondence between the temperature and the time of day. When you go on a trip, the distance you have traveled is a function of the time you have been on the road. The height of a particular child is a function of his or her age.

Although such functions cannot be represented with formulas, the data can be shown in tables and on graphs. Through interpreting the tables and graphs, we can learn more about the phenomena being represented. Is there a tendency toward increase or decrease? When is the increase faster, and when is it slower?

In this chapter, students in Grades 1, 3, and 8 examine functions without formulas and characterize the changes observed.

C A S E   27

How low will it go?

Barbara

GRADE 3, DECEMBER

Since the first day of school, my class has been recording the daily temperature each morning. Every Wednesday we record the temperature data in a table and plot the information on a line graph. In previous years when my class has recorded the temperature, we have not put that data on a graph. By having this year's class create a line graph, students have been able to observe changes over time and to make predictions, which were not so evident just by listing the daily temperature. In former years, the children would notice that the temperatures were all in the 30s or that there had been many days when the temperature was 54 degrees. However, they were not really thinking about the changes. They were not able to easily look at the data over time in order to make reasonable predictions about the changes that were about to happen.

This year, the class has been very interested in examining the line graph representing the weekly temperatures and have been noticing patterns and making predictions since the first week of school. We have now collected 15 weeks of data.

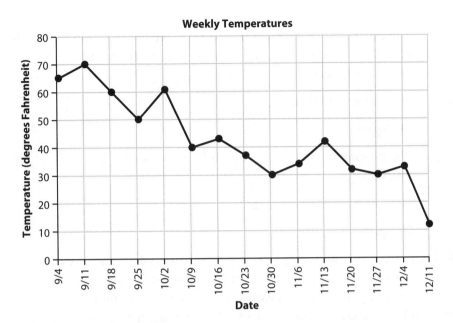

Weekly Temperatures

When we first talked about temperature, it was clear that my students expected the temperature to go down as fall progressed. However, they thought it would always get colder week by week, and the temperature would not rise again until spring. The fact that, even in September, October, and November, the temperature might be warmer than the previous week was hard for some children to wrap their brains around.

Because the temperature went up from the first data collection to the second, then down the third, some students predicted it would continue to go up, down, up, down. It did not. The temperature went down again from the third week to the fourth. Then it went up, so there were many predictions about whether a pattern would appear and what it would be.

The students noticed that at times, the temperature changed a lot within a week. From October 2 to October 9, it dropped 21 degrees, more than the previous weeks.

By late October, students remarked that, even though the temperature was going up and down, it was going down more than it was going up.

On December 11, I passed out copies of our temperature graph. When I asked the children how much the temperature had changed from the previous week, most of them tackled it as a difference problem and easily saw that the temperature was 21 degrees less than the week before. Several described this week's temperature as ⁻21 degrees from the last week.

They were also able to describe the graph and make comparisons between similar changes on the graph.

ROSA: The downs "change" from the fifth day we got the temper- | 40
ature to the sixth day is the same as from the fourteenth to
the fifteenth day.

TEACHER: How much did it change?

JACK: 21 degrees.

BRAD: It's the same on the double down from the second to the | 45
fourth day.

TEACHER: How much was that change?

JOSH: 20 degrees.

This is where we are today. I am enjoying these discussions each week.
More importantly, most children are eager to see what each week's tem- | 50
perature does to our graph. They like making predictions and figuring out
the story that these data are telling us about the changing temperatures.

C A S E 28

Melting snow and ice

Jessica

GRADE 1, JANUARY

This lesson was based on a science experiment comparing the rates at
which packed snow, loose snow, and crushed ice melt.

The experiment was set up using six graduated cylinders. One group | 55
of students put 50 milliliters of loose snow into two of the cylinders. The
second group put 50 milliliters of packed snow into two of the graduated
cylinders. The third group filled their two cylinders with 50 milliliters
of crushed ice. We put all 6 cylinders together on a table and made our
predictions. What would happen? Which would melt first? The students' | 60
predictions were split pretty evenly; 6 thought the loose snow would melt
first; 7 thought the packed snow would melt the quickest, and 6 students
thought ice would be the first to melt. We started recording at 10:00 a.m.;

all cylinders were recorded at a level of 50 milliliters. Then we went back
every 30 minutes to look at the level of the substance in each of the cylin- 65
ders. As the snow and ice melted, the volume of substance in each cylinder
decreased, but at different rates. We recorded our data in a table:

Time	Loose	Packed	Ice
10:00 a.m.	50 ml	50 ml	50 ml
10:30 a.m.	20 ml	40 ml	35 ml
11:00 a.m.	15 ml	31 ml	30 ml
11:30 a.m.	14 ml	31 ml	30 ml
12:00 a.m.	14 ml	31 ml	30 ml

Now, what to do with the information?

The class has worked on pictographs and bar graphs this year. They
have never made a line graph, so we started building one together. I set up 70
the horizontal axis as the time from 10:00 a.m. to 12:00 p.m. and the vertical axis as the amount of snow or ice measured in milliliters from 0 milliliters to 50 milliliters. We color-coded the information using yellow for ice,
pink for packed snow, and blue for loose snow. We plotted the points and
made the lines connecting the dots. 75

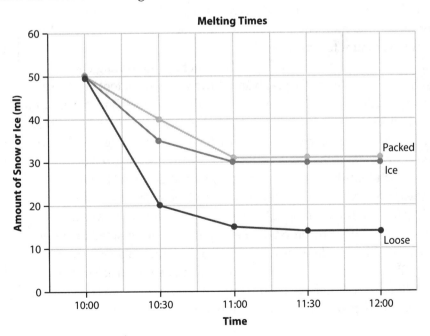

Jessica

GRADE 1, JANUARY

Once the graph was made, I asked if anyone could read it, explain what it showed, and comment on what they noticed about the graph.

As students looked at the first 30 minutes that were represented on the graph, they noticed how long the blue line for loose snow was. This line decreased from 50 milliliters all the way down to 20 milliliters. It decreased much more than the other two lines. Then it continued to decrease to 15 milliliters and then even more to 14 milliliters. The line decreased because the snow was melting. Then the line just went straight across. Why?

It was not long before a few students figured out by looking at the times, 11:30 and 12:00, that it was because the snow was mostly melted by then, and it was not going to change again.

They then started to focus on the lines for the packed snow and the ice. They noted how close the two lines were on the graph. The ice melted a little faster at first, but the packed snow "caught up (almost)" by 11:00. They talked about how close 30 milliliters and 31 milliliters were on the graduated cylinder, and it showed up on the graph with the lines being so close together.

Again they knew that the horizontal lines meant that most of the ice and snow had melted. The big question was, "Why was the loose snow's straight (i.e., horizontal) line down so low and so far away from the other two? After all, they all started with the same amount—or did they?"

Michael explained, "The loose snow didn't have as much snow as the packed snow, even though they both started at 50 milliliters. The loose snow had places where there was air. When we packed down the snow we got rid of the air and more snow fit into those spaces. So they really didn't have the same amount to start with."

Michael came up to me later and said that he noticed something that surprised him. He pointed to the graph and showed me that it took the loose snow longer to melt. Half past eleven was when the horizontal line started, and the other two lines were horizontal at 11:00. He was pretty proud of himself for being the only one to notice this. I told him that was an interesting question to consider: Why did it take the graph of the loose snow longer to even out?

Could my students have made a line graph on their own? Probably not, but I was pleased with the information they were able to obtain from the graph. After the lesson, I thought of a few things I would have done differently. I would have recorded data every 15 minutes instead of every 30 minutes. The snow melted faster than I had thought. I also would have started by filling the cylinders with 100 milliliters of snow or ice rather than 50 milliliters. I might have used the word *slope* when I was discussing the graph, just to expose my students to the term.

The burning candle

Maggie
GRADE 8 SPECIAL NEEDS, DECEMBER

I asked my students to predict how the height of a burning candle would
change over time. Would it melt at a constant rate? How could they tell?
Why might it not melt at a constant rate? I also asked them to take an educated
guess of what the table and graph might look like. They had been looking
at distance versus time graphs, which all had positive slopes, and the corresponding speed versus time graphs. Would my students sense that the shrink-
ing candle would have a negative slope? How would they identify whether or
not the data showed a constant or changing rate of melting? These were some
of the questions I pondered before I presented my students with the problem.

Most students predicted that the height of the candle would not decrease at a constant rate. Several stated that because the candle was nar-
rower at the top and wider at the bottom the top part would burn more
quickly than the bottom. Some felt the changing air currents in the room
might affect the way the candle burned.

Students were then asked to predict what a graph of the situation would
look like. Several of their graphs of height versus time looked like this:

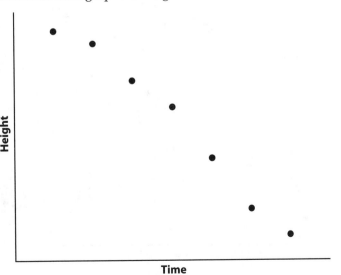

They said it would look like this because the height of the candle would go down as the candle burned. Some made a straight line while others, like Mario, made it curved. The students who curved the line said that it indicated the candle was burning more slowly toward the end.

Some students' predictions looked like this:

135

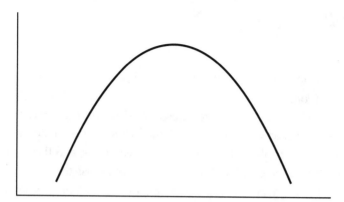

Nathan said that the first increasing slope represents the candle burning more and more quickly; then it reaches a point when the candle starts to burn at a slower rate. I see that Nathan did not label his axes. It seems the graph was not of the *height* of the candle but instead the rate of burning. It resembles some of the graphs of speed we worked on earlier.

140

I also had students who predicted graphs that looked like this:

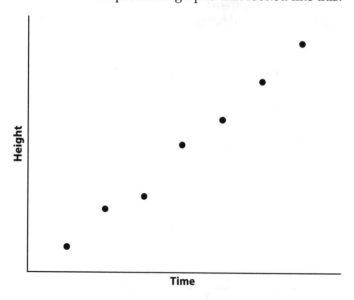

Functions Without Formulas

As Amy created her graph, she started on the right side and methodically made the line go down toward the left. She knows that the height of the candle would go down but for some reason did not start at the left side. Maybe she thinks all graphs go up from left to right.

Joseph predicted the following graph:

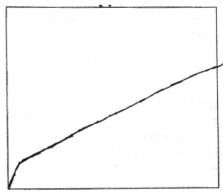

because when you first light it it will burn more quickly because the wax is just starting to melt & then it will start to slow down because the melted wax is slowing it down.

Reading left to right, he described his graph in the following way, "When you first light it, it will burn more quickly because the wax is starting to melt. Then it will start to slow down because the melted wax is slowing it down." This was similar to distance versus time graphs we created when we collected data of the distance traveled over a given period of time. It seems that Joseph has graphed the amount of wax that has melted rather than the height of the candle (the amount of wax remaining).

After students had made their predictions about how the burning candle would melt and sketched out a graph of the situation, I gave each student a 9-centimeter birthday candle and a table to record their data. I asked each of them to record the candle's height every 30 seconds after it was lit. I used a timer and instructed students when to take their measurements. After recording their data, they created the corresponding graphs. All of the students produced graphs of height versus time with a negative slope. Once they had finished their graphs, they responded to questions about their graphs and compared their initial guesses to what they actually found to be true.

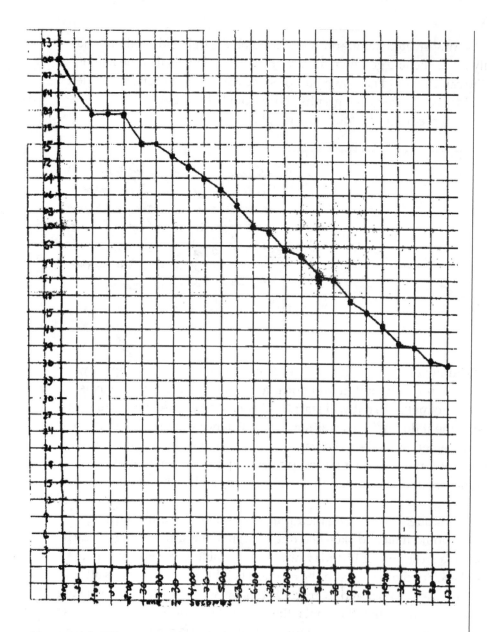

Drew said, "The candle is melting, or going down, but sometimes it burns more quickly than other times." I asked how he could tell when it burned more quickly. He replied, "It goes down steeper, and when it is burning at a slower rate, the graph is not as steep. I think of it like a hill; the steeper the slope, the faster something is going."

165

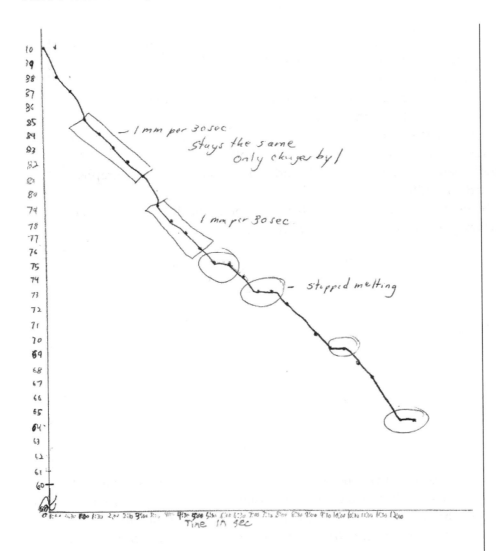

Mario said that he could see the candle melted at a constant rate at certain times. He pointed to a section of the line on his graph that was drawn at a 45 degree angle and said, "This part shows that the candle is melting 1 millimeter every 30 seconds." I asked what it meant when the line on the graph was horizontal. He replied, "The candle stopped melting. Its height didn't change." The graph held a great deal of meaning for him.

Most students made similar observations. They realized that their candles did not burn at a constant rate, but while they were observing, measuring, and recording data, the candle did burn at constant rates for parts of the time. They were able to tell that the rate was 1 millimeter per 30 seconds or 2 or 3 millimeters per 30 seconds by looking at the graph and the slope of the line.   180

Students looked at the difference between the graphs they initially drew and those they made from the data. Amy realized the error in her first graph and explained that she had gone from right to left instead of left to right. Joseph said that in his initial description he was correct, that the   185 candle started out burning quickly and then slowed, but his two graphs looked quite different.

Some students examined their table and found the difference between each measurement. This is what Crissy's table looked like:

Time	Height in mm	
0:00	90	
		5
0:30	85	
		2
1:00	83	
		2
1:30	81	
		2
2:00	79	
		4
2:30	75	
		0
3:00	75	

Crissy explained that when the difference is 2 several times in a row, it   190 is because the candle was melting at a constant rate. (The class has yet to work on the idea that, since the height is decreasing, the difference is noted as negative.) Most students, however, said they felt it was easier to see and interpret the graph for rate of change than it was just to look at the table.

My students learned a lot during this investigation. An interesting   195 follow-up activity would be to give them a written description of something that is changing over time and ask them to create a corresponding table and graph. Would their insights from the melting candle experience transfer to a different situation?

C H A P T E R

8

The Mathematics of Patterns, Functions, and Change for the K–8 Classroom

Stephen Monk, University of Washington

Deborah Schifter, EDC

Tracy Noble, TERC

1 • Overview of the Mathematics of Patterns, Functions, and Change

2 • Patterns and Sequences

3 • Linear Functions

4 • Nonlinear Functions

5 • Data-Based Functions

6 • The Concept of Function

1 • OVERVIEW OF THE MATHEMATICS OF PATTERNS, FUNCTIONS, AND CHANGE

Imagine that you have just opened your telephone bill and among the pieces of paper that hide the actual bill is a glossy red one announcing a "NEW CALLING PLAN—WITH NO MONTHLY FEE!!!" When you read through all the fine print and look at the bill you just received, it appears that they are offering an alternative to your current calling plan. With your current plan,

5

141

which they call the "10 + 10 Plan," you pay a $10.00 monthly fee for long distance service and 10¢ a minute for long-distance calls. Now, with the new "Free & Easy Plan," they do not charge any monthly fee at all, but they charge 15¢ a minute for your calls. The letter included with the bill, from someone with the title "Vice President for Promotional Sales," tells you that based on your current bill, you would have saved $2.85 this month if you had been on the new Free & Easy Plan. However, that is just this month. How can you tell if it would be the better deal during other months?

You like the idea of saving money on your phone bill, so you sit down with a pencil, paper, and a calculator to figure out what your monthly phone bill would be for various numbers of minutes with each of the plans. First you try 150 minutes and find that the bill would be $25.00 with the 10 + 10 Plan and only $22.50 with the Free & Easy Plan. Then you find the cost of 300 minutes of long-distance calling. With the 10 + 10 Plan, the cost for 300 minutes would be $40.00 and with the Free & Easy Plan the cost would be $45.00. Clearly for 300 minutes, you are better off keeping your current plan. What about 175 minutes and 247 minutes? Should you just keep finding the cost for random numbers of minutes? One plan would cost less for some amounts and more for others. This is not like choosing a bag of flour when you know how much flour you want and you can see what the unit cost is for each brand. Here, you are choosing between two plans, and the cost with each plan depends on how you and your family use the phone. How can you compare plans when you do not know how many minutes you will talk?

Putting your calculator aside, you decide to think about the structure of the two plans. The 10 + 10 Plan costs $10 before you make any phone calls at all. Then you save 5¢ over the Free & Easy Plan for each minute you talk. If you talk for a lot of minutes, that 5¢ per minute savings would add up. Wait. That is an idea to try. How many minutes would it take for the savings to add up to the extra $10? That would be 200 minutes. If you talked for 200 minutes on the 10 + 10 Plan, then you would save enough on minutes to balance the $10 monthly fee. So you would do better staying with your 10 + 10 Plan for *any number of minutes greater than 200.* You think your family does use over 200 minutes during most months. But is your reasoning correct? Maybe a graph would be helpful in figuring this out. Then you remember the cases about the Penny Jar and the children collecting marbles. They were somewhat like this telephone bill problem. In each case there was a start number (which could be 0) and an amount that is added in some regular way. The 10 + 10 Plan is similar because it has a start number of $10 and the amount added is 10¢ for each minute of long-distance calling. The Free & Easy Plan has a start number of 0 and the amount added is 15¢ for each minute used.

This example typifies an area in mathematics and a kind of reasoning that is different from arithmetic and yet involves a great deal of arithmetic. The computations express relationships over a range of possible numbers and not just a few specific numbers. In that way, it seems like the algebra you studied in school. Yet, this problem can be solved without using the most prominent feature of school algebra—formulas involving variables like x and y. The mathematical concept at the core of this problem is a relationship between quantities. In the telephone plan problem, there are two different relationships to be compared. They are both of the form: "If you are calling long distance for a certain number of minutes, then you have to pay a certain amount of money." Using formulas involving variables such as x and y is just one approach to addressing this problem. However, there are other types of representations, including diagrams, concrete materials, words, tables, and graphs. As you will see from the examples in this essay and have already seen in the seminar, each type of representation has its own characteristics.

This essay addresses a set of ideas that form a central area of study in algebra, the analysis of certain relationships between quantities, called "functions." The long-distance phone bill problem illustrates many of the main issues and ideas in this area.

■ Knowing the value of one quantity (in the telephone example, number of minutes) enables us to determine the value of the other quantity (the cost of this many minutes for a particular plan). However, there are many possible values for the quantities, so it is inefficient or impossible to simply list them all. We must reason about a wide range of possible values of one quantity and the resulting value of the other.

■ There are many ways to represent the information in the problem. We could make a list of possible number of minutes on the phone and the resulting phone bill; we could make a more formal table of values that systematizes the list. We could make a graph or a diagram, or we could reason verbally about the situation. We could also create a formula that describes the relationship between number of minutes and the size of the bill.

■ There is logic to the situation. There are underlying patterns in the relationship between values of time on the phone and the corresponding costs. ("If you talked for 200 minutes on the 10 + 10 Plan, then you would save enough on minutes to balance the $10 monthly fee." "For every minute you talk beyond 200 minutes, the 10 + 10 plan saves you 5¢.") These relational analyses, and not the particulars of one specific amount of time and its resulting cost, are the key to solving the problem.

There are three general families of functions that are studied in the Patterns, Functions, and Change seminar. The first family consists of relationships characterized by constant rate of change. The telephone bill problem is an example of this type of function. In the 10 + 10 Plan, every time you talk for an additional 50 minutes, your bill increases by $5.

Minutes	Cost (in dollars)
0	10
50	15
100	20
150	25
200	30
250	35

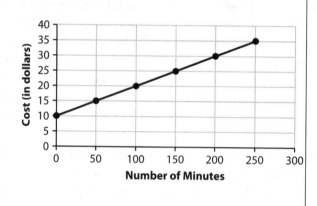

Because the points in the table lie along a straight line when graphed, this function is identified as a *linear function*. Many situations that appear in the Casebook, such as those involving the Staircase Towers, lunch money, and the crayfish race, present examples of linear functions.

The second family consists of functions that are defined by formulas but are not linear. That is, the change is predictable but the rate of change is not constant, and the graph does not appear as a straight line. An example of this second type of function is the relationship between the area of a square and the length of a side. For any length of side, we can determine the area of the square. However, when the side increases from 1 to 2 inches, the area increases by 3 square inches (from 1 to 4), but when the side increases from 6 to 7 inches (still an increase of 1 inch), the area increases by 13 square inches (from 36 to 49). The graph of this function gently curves upward. Nonlinear relationships defined by formulas are explored in the Casebook, Chapter 6, Cases 23–26.

Length of Sides in Inches	Area in Square Inches
1	1
2	4
3	9
4	16
5	25
6	36
7	49
8	64

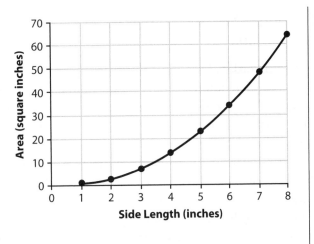

The third family of functions consists of *data-based* relationships in which two quantities vary but are *not* related by any known formula. Even though these relationships cannot be defined by an algebraic rule, they are still functions. Students in the Casebook, Chapter 7, Cases 27–29, examine such functions: how temperature changes over time, how the volume of a substance in a beaker changes as that substance melts, or how the height of a candle changes as it burns. These phenomena, while not bound by formulas, can be represented by tables and graphs and analyzed with methods similar to those used with linear and nonlinear functions. Of particular interest is how changes in temperature or height are expressed in tables and graphs.

The examples in each of these families of relationships share the important feature that they are built around a correspondence between concrete quantities in real situations—of money, time, temperature, height, etc. Because so many situations can be described in terms of such relationships, it became useful for mathematicians to develop a concept that is built around correspondences. This is the origin of the mathematical concept of *function*.

Some of the ideas of functions can be rooted in students' early work with patterns and sequences. Thus, this essay begins here, with a section on patterns and sequences. It then discusses each of the three families of functions, a section dedicated to each. It concludes with a final section on the concept of function.

2 • PATTERNS AND SEQUENCES *Patterns and sequences can provide the basis of the study of functions.*

Sequences, an ordered list of items, involve the most basic patterns. One of the ways in which number sequences are of interest to mathematicians is that they can have various arithmetic relationships among their terms. One might say that the sequence 1, 3, 5, 7, 9, 11 is not very different from the list *a, c, e, g, i, k, m*, in that both consist of the alternate elements in standard lists, the first the list of the counting numbers and the second the list of the letters in alphabetical order. What makes the number sequence different from the list of letters is that we can talk about arithmetic combinations and relations among the terms of that sequence. For instance, if we subtract any term in this sequence from its successor, then we always get a difference of 2. However, no such statement can be made about a list of letters. Working with numbers and not letters also enables us to define a sequence using arithmetic formulas. I can communicate to others what I have in mind when I am thinking of the sequence 1, 4, 9, 16, 25, 36, ... by saying that the terms of the sequence I am thinking of are $1 \times 1, 2 \times 2, 3 \times 3, 4 \times 4, 5 \times 5, 6 \times 6$, ... or equivalently, $1^2, 2^2, 3^2$, and so forth. This is not possible with letters or other elements on which I cannot perform arithmetic operations.

A significant feature of such number sequences is their predictability. Once you know the rule that defines the sequence, you can say what value will be 8 terms ahead or what will appear in the 25th position. However, as Case 1, "Patterns on the pocket chart," shows, our ability to determine what is ahead is not restricted to number sequences. Soon after kindergartners recognize that the pattern of animal tracks presented by their teacher is an *a, b, a, b* pattern (cat, dog, cat, dog), they determine that the track in the 8th position must be that of a dog.

This kind of exploration of non-numerical patterns can provide the foundation for later work on numerical patterns (English & Warren, 1998). The transition from non-numerical to numerical patterns is made more explicit in Case 4, "Four-element repeating patterns." Here, the students are working with a train of colored cubes organized in the repeating pattern: red, blue, yellow, green, red, blue, yellow, green. These students find various strategies to answer such questions as, What color is the 16th cube? What positions do the blue cubes hold? The latter question invites students to generate a numerical sequence: 2, 6, 10, 14, ..., which they can explore further. Their understanding of the pattern's unit—red, blue, yellow, green—helps them to see what is common among a set of sequences, all generated by the different color cubes.

135

140

145

150

155

160

165

170

The type of sequence generated by the color-cube problem is so common it has a name: arithmetic progression. To form an arithmetic progression, you start with any number a, and then add the number d to get $a + d$, and then add the number d again to get $a + 2d$, and then add the number d again to get $a + 3d$. The students in Case 4 generate a sequence that starts with 2 and then successively add 4 to each resulting term. The students in Case 2, working with Staircase Towers (e.g., begin with a tower of 1 cube and go up 2 cubes with each step), and in Case 3 with Penny Jars (e.g., begin with 2 pennies in the penny jar and add 3 pennies each day) also create arithmetic progressions.

A sequence appears to involve just one quantity. However, any number in a sequence has a place in that sequence. A number might represent the 1st, 2nd, or 12th term in that sequence. Thus, you can always construct a relationship between any sequence and the counting numbers. For example, you can construct a quantitative relationship between two quantities based on staircase towers (start with 1; step up 2 each time) in which the 1st tower is 1 cube; the 2nd tower is 3 cubes; the 3rd tower is 5 cubes; etc.

Position in the Sequence	Number of Cubes in the Tower
1	1
2	3
3	5
4	7
5	9
6	11
7	13

3 • LINEAR FUNCTIONS *A linear function is characterized by a constant rate of change.*

Linear functions are typified by the telephone plan, the Penny Jar, and the Magic Marbles. In these contexts, you start with some amount (which can be 0) and then add a constant amount over equal intervals. Any arithmetic progression, viewed as a correspondence between the position of a term and its value, is a linear function.

Consider a Penny Jar situation with a start number of 10 pennies and with 4 pennies added each day. The amount after 1 day would be expressed as 10 + 4; after 2 days the amount would be expressed as 10 + 2(4); after 3 days, 10 + 3(4). To generate a formula for the number of pennies in the jar, we could say 10 + d(4) in which the letter d is chosen to stand for any possible value for the number of days of collecting pennies.

In addition to using algebraic expressions to describe these relationships, we can represent them using tables. Notice that the table below includes an entry for the 10-penny start number. Notice, too, each time d increases by 1, p, the number of pennies in the jar, increases by a constant amount—the defining characteristic of all linear functions.

d (days)	p (pennies)
0	10
1	14
2	18
3	22
4	26
5	30
6	34
7	38
8	42
9	46
10	50
11	54
12	58
13	62

A graph of this Penny Jar situation is shown below. Although the Penny Jar graph is actually a series of discrete points representing the number of pennies in the jar on Day 1, Day 2, etc., it is helpful to connect the points to see what trend they indicate.

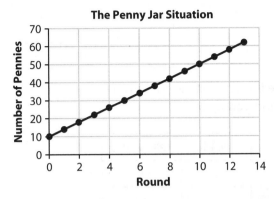

The Penny Jar Situation

The value of the function that corresponds to $d = 0$ (in which the graph intersects the y-axis) is called the "y-intercept." The amount of increase each day is referred to as the "slope."

3 • 1 Conventional representations of quantitative relationships *Conventional representations convey information in a standard and compact form.*

Before continuing discussion of linear functions, let us note their variety of representations, including tables, algebraic expressions, and graphs. Each of these commonly used modes of representation is organized to convey a great deal of information in compact form. However, that is precisely what makes them so challenging to learn to use. This section discusses some of the conventions governing three types of representation, referring to both the mathematics education research literature and the cases to illustrate these challenges.

3.1.1 • Tables *Tables are ordered lists of values of two (or more) variables.*
Two quantities are represented in each of the functions explored thus far in the essay: the number of days that pennies have been collecting in a jar and the number of pennies in the jar, the number of minutes a family talks on the phone in a month and the charges that appear on the monthly bill. The number of pennies in the jar depends on the numbers of days you have been collecting them; the charges on the bill depend on the number of minutes your family members talk on the phone. In order to distinguish between the two quantities in any particular situation, one is called the *input value* or *independent variable* (*variable* because the quantity varies), the other, the *output value* or *dependent variable*. With tables written vertically, the input value is conventionally placed in the left column and the output value in the right.

In Case 10, "Multiple formulas for blue and yellow tiles," Drew works on the correspondence between blue and yellow tiles in a set of figures that grows according to a particular pattern.

215

220

225

230

235

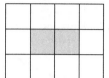 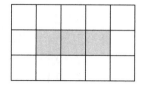

To begin to explore this context, he creates a table to record corresponding numbers of blue and yellow tiles.

Blue Tiles	Yellow Tiles
1	8
2	10
3	12
4	14
5	16
6	18
7	20
8	22
9	24
10	26

Drew describes the relationship of blue to yellow tiles: "Every time we go to the next level of blue, there are always 2 more yellow tiles." When the teacher asks him to compare what happens to the blue tiles with what happens to the yellow tiles, he says, "As blue goes up 1, yellow goes up 2."

Drew goes on to devise a formula that expresses the number of yellow tiles in terms of the number of blue tiles. That is, the number of yellow tiles can be determined by the formula $2n + 6$, where n stands for any number of blue tiles. Thus, for any number, n, in the left column of the table, the expression $2n + 6$ gives the number in the right column.

Drew looks at the table in two directions: down the columns to see how the variation in one quantity is related to the variation in the other, a strategy that produces a "recursive" rule; across the columns to see how the input value translates into the output value, producing a "closed form" rule. Confrey and Smith (1994, 1995) have found that, even when students are asked to find the correspondence between two variables in closed form, they spontaneously explore numerical patterns in both directions, which helps them to better understand the function. The recursive rule makes particularly prominent the way the output value changes as the input value changes.

In Case 5, "Making sense of tables," as the students are just beginning to learn to use tables, they are also exploring a new context. In this second-grade class, their task is to build "buildings" out of cubes, each "floor" consisting of 3 "rooms," then to record the growing number of floors and rooms in a table. Although the table organizes information in a clear and concise way, the second graders find it difficult to keep track of the relationship between floors and rooms while also sorting out the table's structure. The teacher concluded that it would have been helpful for students to spend some time finding their own ways to keep track of the buildings, so that they would understand the purpose of the tables, before she introduced a standard format for making a table.

3.1.2 • Algebraic expressions *Many functions can be expressed as an algebraic formula defining the output value (dependent variable) in terms of the input value (independent variable).*

The Penny Jar begins with 10 pennies in the jar; when 4 pennies are added each day, the number of pennies in the jar, p, is equal to $10 + (d \times 4)$. In fact, any letters can be chosen for the two variables as long as each variable is clearly defined. Frequently, x is chosen for the independent variable y for the dependent variable. (That is, we could choose to write the Penny Jar rule as $y = 10 + (x \times 4)$.) When possible values for the independent variable are whole numbers, the letter n is often chosen.

We have seen that any linear function is defined by two elements: the value of the output when the input value is 0 (also called the *y-intercept*) and the increment of the output value when the input value increases by 1 (called the *slope*). When those two elements have not been specified, a linear function expressed algebraically is $y = mx + b$, where b is the y-intercept and m is the slope. Written in this form, the Penny Jar situation is $p = 4d + 10$; the slope is 4 and the y-intercept is 10.

Equivalent forms of expressing this relationship—$p = 4d + 10$ and $p = 10 + d4$, among others—are equally valid. In fact, Erick Smith (2003) has found that, rather than always using the form $y = mx + b$, students tend to prefer the algebraic expression that best describes the actions in the problem situation. In Case 10, "Multiple formulas for blue and yellow tiles," Drew demonstrates that by decomposing the blue and yellow tiles in different ways, he can produce three equivalent expressions to represent the correspondence between the two variables: $2n + 6$, $2(n + 2) + 2$, and

$3(n + 2) - n$. As he moves between the use of tiles and the algebraic expressions, Drew deepens his understanding of both forms of representation and of the connections between them.

3.1.3 • Graphs *A graph provides a visual representation of a function.*

The third graders in Case 8, "Graphing staircase problems," the seventh graders in Case 9, "Making sense of coordinate graphs," and the fourth graders in Case 16, "Collecting bottles," are learning how to use graphs to visually represent functions but have not yet mastered the process of graphing. Their work highlights some of the possibilities and challenges of representing data visually, as well as the role of conventions in graphing.

For example, in Case 16, some of the fourth graders work on a problem about children collecting bottles for a charity. They were asked to think about which student brought the most bottles after two weeks, given that

1. Zelda started out with 30 bottles and brought in 2 bottles every day.
2. Mario started out with 10 bottles and brought in 5 bottles every day.
3. Anna started out with 40 bottles and brought in 1 bottle every day.
4. Ben did not have any bottles at home to start, but then he brought in 8 bottles every day.

When they were asked to graph the bottles each student brought, some students created simple bar graphs, in which the final number of bottles collected by each student was represented but not the number of bottles brought each day.

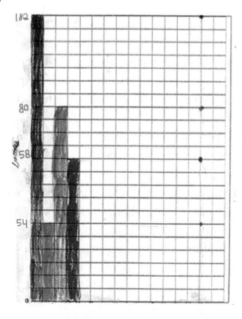

While the student whose work is shown here did not create the graph the teacher had expected, she did create a graph that represented the number of bottles each student collected (although the student does need to attend to the scale on the y-axis), showing the answer to the question, Who collected the most bottles? In some circumstances, a bar graph might be exactly the kind of graph needed, and experienced graph-users can make many different types of graphs to represent the same situation, depending on what they wish to highlight. The teacher asked additional questions of the student who made this graph, to challenge her to represent the number of bottles collected each day by each student. Some other students in the class did create graphs representing the number of bottles each student had collected at each point in time, which allowed one to see not only who collected the most bottles but also how fast each student collected bottles and by how much a student was ahead at any given time. The various types of graphs students created for the "Collecting bottles" situation illustrates the diversity of features of the situation that were important to each of them and the various ways the same situation can be represented in graphical form.

Nemirovsky and Tierney (2001) reviewed many years of work with elementary school students to try to better understand why they sometimes create unexpected or unconventional graphs. They found that these students are not making random errors nor are necessarily unfamiliar with conventions. Instead, students create the graphs they do in order to represent the aspects of the situation that are important to them and relevant to the story the data represents, like the student in the "Collecting bottles" case. Of course, this is what graphs are for—to represent a mathematical situation in meaningful ways.

Yet it is important for students to learn the conventions. After all, standard conventions of graphing make it easier to communicate meaning to others. Nemirovsky and Tierney suggest two ways of helping students learn these without losing sight of the meaningfulness of this representation. First, teachers can suggest that certain components be removed from the graph or added to the graph. For instance, the teacher in the "Collecting bottles" case suggested to the student who made the bar graph that she extend her graph over time, adding a new component to her representation. The second suggestion offered by Nemirovsky and Tierney is that students be asked to share their graphs with others; the goal of communicating often brings out the need for common conventions of representation.

In Case 8, "Graphing staircase problems," the third graders had such an opportunity when their teacher asked them to compare pairs of graphs to each other. While all the students in this case graphed their values for the number of cubes in each staircase tower as points with coordinates (x, y), they had not yet learned the convention that the input value appears on the x-axis, the output value on the y-axis. Thus, some students put the input value on the x-axis and some on the y-axis; two of the graphs of the same situation held up next to each other had different slants because the two students had used different conventions for which variable is on which axis. In this case, the class had an opportunity to see the value of using a consistent rule for which variable goes on which axis, because when students made different choices about this, their graphs were difficult to compare.

Note that many of the situations in the Casebook involve discrete variables. For example, the input value for the Penny Jar situations takes on the values 0, 1, 2, 3, 4, ... but not 1.5 or $\sqrt{3}$. That is, when the input value is number of rounds, it takes on only whole number values. Thus, the graph of the Penny Jar, start with 10 and add 4 each round, is actually a discrete set of points.

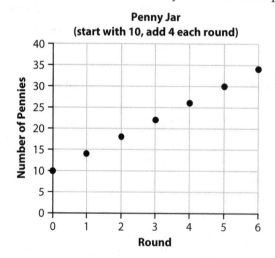

Knowing that the graph of this function is a set of discrete points, sometimes we connect the points to reveal a trend. For example, when we connect the points for this Penny Jar situation, we find that all the points lie on a straight line.

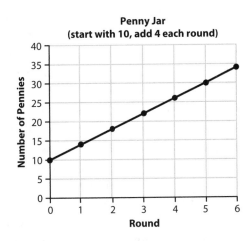

Penny Jar
(start with 10, add 4 each round)

Sometimes, especially when we know the formula for the function, we become interested in the continuous function in which the Penny Jar is embedded. For example, knowing the formula $y = 4x + 10$, we may now be interested in the function whose input takes on all the values of the number line. Now the graph is a continuous straight line that extends indefinitely in both directions.

380

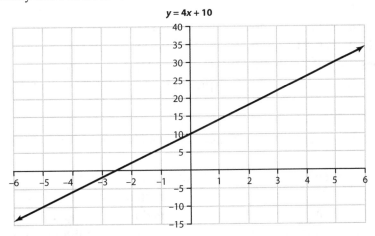

$y = 4x + 10$

In addition to tables, algebraic expressions, and graphs, the Casebook describes students using many other forms of representation. For example, students use cubes to represent lunches and lunch money (Case 6, "Lunch money models"), pictures of pennies in a penny jar (Case 7, "Penny Jar arrays"), tiles decomposed in different ways (Case 10, "Multiple formulas for blue and yellow tiles"), and number lines to show the movement of crayfish in a crayfish race (Case 14, "The crawling crayfish"), to mention a

385

few. The pedagogical value of using a variety of means to represent mathematical relationships is supported by many studies (Borba & Confrey, 1996; Confrey & Smith, 1995; Healy & Hoyles, 1999; Kaput, 1989; Monk, 2003; Moschkovich et al., 1993; Noble et al., 2001, 2002; Zazkis et al., 1996), as well as the NCTM Standards (2000). Confrey and Smith (2001) argue that "each representation yields its own insights" into mathematical relationships and that no representation can on its own be seen as conveying all the mathematical meaning of such a relationship.

Noble et al. (2001) explored in detail how two fifth-grade students used multiple representations of a race in which two people were moving at different constant rates. (The situation was similar to the crayfish race in Case 14.) The fifth graders' representations included a number table and a graph, as well as Cuisenaire rods moving down a track and a computer simulation of the race (Tierney et al., 1998). Noble et al. found what Confrey and Smith would have predicted, namely that different representations highlighted different features of the linear functions. For instance, the number table highlighted the multiplicative relationship between distance and time, while the action with the Cuisenaire rods highlighted the gradual pulling away of one racer from the other. Focusing on one representation alone would not have allowed for this diversity of ways of understanding the linear relationships these students were exploring. The cases in this Casebook also illustrate how students' use of multiple representations helps them to deepen their understandings of the relationships between variables and to interpret the conventional forms of representation.

3.2 • Linear functions and constant rate of change *Constant rate of change produces a straight line graph.*

As explained above, one property shared by all linear functions is a constant rate of change. For instance, in the Penny Jar situation, if 3 days go by, then the same number of pennies is added, whether we consider Day 1 to Day 4 or Day 14 to Day 17. Similarly, when constructing a building with the same number of rooms on each floor, each time a floor is added, the same number of rooms is added, no matter if we go from 2 floors to 3 or from 8 floors to 9. In all linear relationships, if you increase the input value by a constant amount, then there is a constant amount by which the output value increases, *regardless of where you are in the range of possible values.*

Examining this property on a graph explains why relationships with this property must have graphs that are straight lines. Suppose A and A'

and *B* and *B'* are pairs of points that represent the same amount of change in the quantity on the horizontal axis; for instance, *A* to *A'* might be from 1 to 4 days and *B* to *B'* might be from 14 to 17 days. The distance we move along the vertical axis from *B* to *B'* must be the same as the distance we move along the vertical axis from *A* to *A'*. That is what makes the graph a straight line and that is why we call such relationships linear. The *slope* of the line is the vertical change divided by the corresponding horizontal change.

430

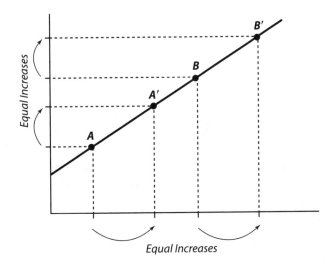

As we saw in Case 8, "Graphing staircase problems," third-grade students were able to discuss the various slopes of their graphs of the number of cubes in a sequence of towers. Students were able to note that one graph was "more up" than another graph when it had a steeper slope. Researchers have found that students of a range of ages perceive and describe differences in slope and can develop this ability and use it to understand how a steeper slope can indicate a greater rate of change (Billings & Lakatos, 2003; Monk & Tierney, in press; Nemirovsky, Tierney, & Wright, 1998).

435

440

Once it is clear that the graph of a linear relationship is a straight line, making the decision between the two plans for long-distance calling is much simpler than one might have imagined. As shown below, the line representing the cost with the Free & Easy Plan is lower for the first 200 minutes, which means that if you talk for less than 200 minutes, then the Free & Easy Plan is cheaper. At 200 minutes, the lines cross. This intersection indicates that if the family talks for exactly 200 minutes, their phone bill will be the same, regardless of the chosen plan. For minutes beyond

445

450

200, the line representing the 10 + 10 Plan is lower, indicating that if you talk for more than 200 minutes, then the 10 + 10 Plan is cheaper.

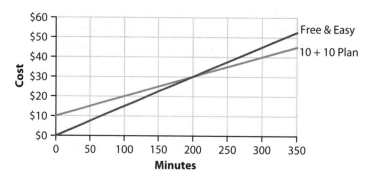

Similarly, in Case 15, "Can Bolar catch up?" the students determine that Franick has more marbles until Day 15, when Bolar catches up, and from then on Bolar has more. In Case 14, "The crawling crayfish," students apply the same kinds of reasoning when they determine that although Flicker starts 10 centimeters ahead, Big Claw catches up after 25 seconds and ultimately wins the race.

3.3 • Direct proportions *When two quantities are directly proportional, they form a special kind of linear function.*
Consider the mathematical relationship between the number of eyes in a room and the number of people in that room. No matter how many people there are, there are twice as many eyes as people (assuming that each person has two eyes). Assuming everyone has 10 toes, there are 10 times as many toes as people, and 10 times as many toes as mouths. So knowing the number of mouths in the room, one can determine the number of toes by multiplying the number of mouths by 10. Knowing how many toes there are and wanting to know how many mouths there are, you simply divide the number of toes by 10.

This kind of relationship is so common that one may tend to take it for granted. It is basic to varying the size of a recipe such as one for salad dressing in which 3 tablespoons of olive oil are combined with 2 tablespoons of vinegar. This relationship between olive oil and vinegar remains the same whether you use exactly these quantities or make enough salad dressing for the school picnic in which case you might use 30 tablespoons of olive oil to 20 tablespoons of vinegar. You can even use 3 pints of olive oil to 2 pints of vinegar or 3 tank cars of olive oil to 2 tank cars of vinegar. It would taste the same. The ratio of olive oil to vinegar is always the same; it is always 3 to 2. This kind of relationship, in which the ratio between the two quantities remains constant, is called a "direct proportion."

480

The students in Case 6, "Lunch money models," use cubes to represent a direct proportion between the number of lunches ordered and the amount of lunch money collected. In Case 17, "5- and 10-floor buildings," students construct "buildings" from cubes, each "floor" with an equal number of "rooms." Here, too, the relationship between the number of rooms in a building and the number of floors is a direct proportion: five rooms per floor produces a 5:1 ratio. The formula that relates r, the number of rooms in a building, to f, the number of floors, is $r = 5f$.

485

f	r
1	5
2	10
3	15
4	20

Notice that quantities that are directly proportional always form linear functions. Each time the input value increases by 1 (e.g., add 1 floor to a building), the output value increases by a constant amount (5 rooms are added). The special characteristic of these linear functions is that the y-intercept (the output value corresponding to an input of 0) is always 0. The slope of the line is the same as the ratio between corresponding values (output to input).

490

495

One of the most important properties of a direct proportion is that if one of the quantities is multiplied by a fixed amount, then the other quantity is also multiplied by that same amount. So, for example, if you know the number of rooms in 4 floors of the building, you can double that number to find the number of rooms in 8 floors of the building. If you double the amount of olive oil in a recipe, then you will have to double the amount of vinegar. This is true, regardless of whether it is for salad dressing with its 3 to 2 ratio or for a cold vegetable soup that takes 3 tablespoons of olive oil to 4 tablespoons of vinegar. Whatever the ratio between two quantities, if one of the quantities is doubled, then the other must also be doubled. However, doubling is just a special case of multiplying; in a direct proportion, this property is true when multiplying by any number.

500

505

If you decide that you want to multiply the amount of vinegar you use in salad dressing by 3 or 6 or even 1.25, then you should also multiply the amount of olive oil by 3 or 6 or 1.25.

The students in Case 17, "5- and 10-floor buildings," and in Case 18, "Cookies and candies," are beginning to recognize just such a relationship. To show how she knows the number of rooms for 10 floors is double the number of rooms for 5 floors, one student, Karen, holds up two 5-floor buildings and puts one on top of the other to create a 10-floor building.

However, once such a relationship is recognized, it is frequently over-generalized. In Case 21, "What's the formula? revisited," students are working with the following growing pattern.

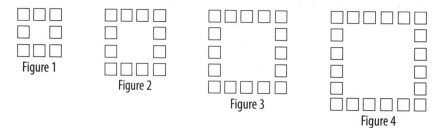

Figure 1

Figure 2

Figure 3

Figure 4

Sheila and Fran correctly determine that to find the number of tiles in a figure, you multiply 4 times the number of tiles on a side (2 more than the figure number) and then subtract 4, because the corner tiles were counted twice. Thus, Figure 20 has 84 tiles; Figure 50 has 204 tiles. The formula for this relationship can be written as $4(n + 2) - 4$, or equivalently, $4n + 4$, where n is the figure number.

However, some of their classmates use a doubling strategy incorrectly. Kevin determines that Figure 10 would have 44 tiles and then argues, "If Figure 10 had 44 tiles, then add 44 more tiles for a total of 88 to get the number of tiles in Figure 20." Similarly, Benito believes that because Figure 25 uses 104 tiles, he can just double to get the number of tiles for Figure 50, 208. Note that both answers are off by 4. This "doubling" error is very common, as both MacGregor and Stacy (1993) and Orton and Orton (1994) report.

In Case 22, "Penny Jar revisited," some students discover that they can use a doubling strategy if they compensate for it. In this lesson, the given situation is: The Penny Jar started with 2 pennies in it. Each round, 5 more pennies are added. Students find that after 5 rounds, there are 27 pennies in the jar. Lynn then says that, in order to solve for Round 10, she doubled the number of pennies after Round 5 ($2 \times 27 = 54$) and then subtracted the start number ($54 - 2$) = 52. She explains, "The 27

510

515

520

525

530

535

pennies from Round 5 already includes the start number. When you double it, you have two start numbers in your total, and so you have to take one out." We see here that it is possible for students to generalize their doubling strategies when they recognize that they need to compensate for doubling the starting amount.

Let us return to the scenario involving the two telephone plans described at the beginning of this essay. While both are examples of linear functions, the Free & Easy Plan is also an example of a direct proportion. If you double the number of minutes you talk, you double the bill; for example, 150 minutes of calls costs $22.50 and 300 minutes costs $45.00. However, because the 10 + 10 plan has a fixed fee this is not the case: 150 minutes would cost $25.00 and 300 minutes would cost $40.00. Applying Lynn's reasoning, if you double the cost for 150 minutes to get $50.00, you have included the $10.00 fixed fee twice. Subtract that out, and you get back to the $40.00 cost for 300 minutes.

4 • Nonlinear Functions *Different categories of nonlinear functions can be characterized by the way change occurs.*

The seminar presents several examples of nonlinear functions: The number of tiles in a square depends on the length of the side of a square; the number of sections a piece of paper is divided into depends on the number of times it has been folded in half; the contribution each person makes to a $36 gift depends on the number of contributors. In all of these relationships, the rate of change in the output value is not constant.

For example, when 2 people contribute to a $36 gift, they each pay $18; when 3 people contribute, each pays $12; 4 people, $9 each. The change in the cost per person as the number of contributers increases from 2 to 3 is $6, and the change from 3 to 4 is $3. As the number of contributors increases by 1, the change is not constant but varies. Examining the ways rates of change vary among nonlinear functions allows us to categorize some of these functions. In this essay, we examine two of these categories, quadratic and exponential relationships.

4.1 • Quadratic functions *In quadratic relationships, the rate of change varies at a constant rate.*
In several of the cases, students work with arrangements of tiles and count the number of tiles needed as some aspect of the arrangement changes. In Case 26, "Playing with squares," students are investigating patterns involved with growing squares.

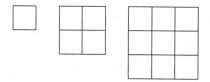

Notice that the number of tiles in each arrangement is the result of multiplying the number of tiles in a side by itself, or, as we say, the number of tiles in the arrangement is the *square* of the number of tiles in a side. The term *square* as used in this situation comes from the fact that we are making square figures. The area of a square with side *m* inches is $m \times m$, or m^2, square inches. This relationship between the number of tiles in the side of the square and the number of tiles required to cover the square is called a *quadratic* relationship. (The root, *quad*, of this term is the Latin word for the number four and refers to four-sided figures.)

The students in Case 26, "Playing with squares," generate the following table from the square arrangements of tiles.

Size of One Side	Number of Tiles
1	1
2	4
3	9
4	16
5	25
6	36
7	49
8	64
9	81
10	100

It is interesting to note that the students in Case 25, "How many outfits?" working in a completely different context, generate the same table. (Here, students found the number of clothing combinations that can be made from *n* different shirts and *n* different pairs of pants.) In both cases, students notice an interesting pattern in the changes of the output value:

As the inputs increase by 1, the changes in output are not constant but form an increasing number sequence, 3, 5, 7, 9, 11, ...

Size of One Side	Number of Tiles Used	
1	1	⟩ +3
2	4	⟩ +5
3	9	⟩ +7
4	16	⟩ +9
5	25	⟩ +11
6	36	⟩ +13
7	49	⟩ +15
8	64	⟩ +17
9	81	⟩ +19
10	100	

595

The reason for this pattern of increase in the number of tiles used in the growing square arrangements can be seen in the following diagram. Each square arrangement fits into the next. To produce the next arrangement, tiles are added to the border along the bottom and the right edge. In producing an arrangement that has k tiles along each side, from an arrangement that has $k - 1$ tiles along each side, we must add k tiles on the bottom and $k - 1$ tiles along the right edge. Altogether, we add $2k - 1$ tiles. This is what the table tells us, because when $k = 2$, we added 3 to the previous number to get 4, when $k = 3$, we added 5 to the previous number to get 9, and so forth.

600

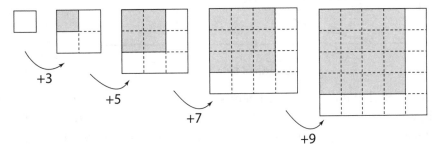

This property of steadily growing increases is shared by many of these growing tile patterns and characterizes a quadratic relationship. As inputs increase by 1, the *change* in output forms a linear function.

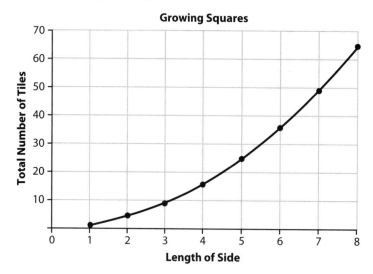

The graph of Growing Squares is increasing and gently curving upward. The upward curve is due to the growth pattern in the dependent variable as the independent variable takes the values 1, 2, 3, ...

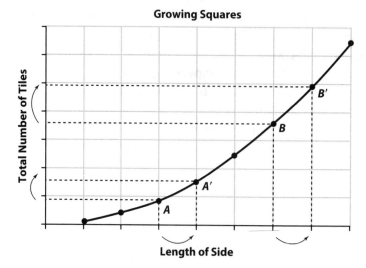

We can reason that the graph must gently curve upward in the same manner in which we were able to see that the graph of a linear function must necessarily be straight—by looking at the pattern of corresponding

changes in the output value as we move along the graph. As is apparent, *A* 615
and *A'* and *B* and *B'* are pairs of points that represent the same amount of
change on the horizontal axis. Because *B* and *B'* are further out along the
graph than *A* and *A'*, the distance we move along the vertical axis from *B*
and *B'* is greater than the vertical distance from *A* to *A'*.

In Case 23, "Fastwalker," students work with a different quadratic relationship. In an imaginary world, an animal called Fastwalker grows 1 centimeter
in the first year of its life, 2 centimeters in the second year, 3 centimeters in the 620
third year, etc. The students graph the relationship and describe what they see.

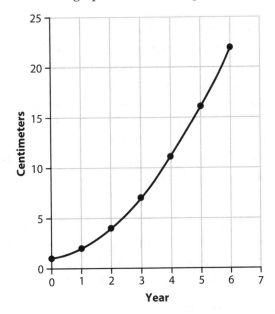

GEOFF: When it goes further, it gets more straight up. The higher
           the number, the more it goes up. It's going up more than it's
           going sideways.

JACK: The numbers are changing. It's not straight because it doesn't 625
           grow at a steady rate.

SANDY: Each time we're adding bigger numbers. It's small at the
           beginning. But, then it's spread out because the numbers are
           bigger. There's more distance between points.

JOSH: The higher the number, the more it goes up. 630

The variety of ways these third graders talk about Fastwalker's graph
is typical of students working to relate visual aspects of the graph with the

numerical data they plot (Noble et al. 2001, 2004; Tierney & Monk, 2007). "More straight up," "not straight," "doesn't grow at a steady rate," "more distance between points," "the more it goes up"—these are all expressions that describe and explain the upward curve of the graph. They reveal that students have a sense of how to perceive the slope of a line and can use this to understand that the slope is changing for this function.

In your work in Session 6, you may have found the formula for the Fastwalker function—$y = 0.5x^2 + 0.5x + 1$, where x is Fastwalker's age in years and y is its height in centimeters. The x^2 term is a characteristic of all quadratic functions. That is, the general form of a quadratic function is $y = ax^2 + bx + c$, where a, b, and c are any numbers on the number line, with $a \neq 0$.

In the math activity of Session 7, you were given a situation of keys dropping from a building and matched it to a graph of height over time that was curving downward. This context is, in fact, another example of a quadratic function. In the 17th century, Galileo determined that when an object is dropped from a height, the distance it has fallen is proportional to the square of the time it has been falling. The formula for the height (in feet) of keys dropped from a 400-foot building is $400 - 16t^2$, in which t is the number of seconds the keys have been falling.

Consider the formulas for the quadratic functions discussed in this section:

- The area of a square as a function of the length of the side: $y = x^2$
- The height of Fastwalker as a function of its age: $y = 0.5x^2 + 0.5x + 1$
- The height of a key dropped from a 400-foot building as a function of the number of seconds it has been falling: $y = 400 - 16t^2$

Although each of the contexts makes sense only for positive values, we can remove the formulas from the context and consider them as defining functions for all the numbers on a number line. Their graphs may now extend into other quadrants of the coordinate plane.

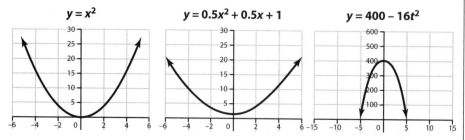

The shape of these graphs, like cups opening up or down, characterizes all quadratic functions.

Note that, even though a quadratic relationship, such as $y = x^2$, might include the point (0, 0), it does not have the doubling property. When $x = 3$, $y = 9$, but when $x = 6$ (the double of 3), $y = 36$ (which is not the double of 9). The doubling property applies only to quantities that are directly proportional, which form a special kind of linear function.

4.2 • Exponential functions *Exponential functions are formed by repeated multiplication.*

Among the functions discussed in the cases that are neither linear nor quadratic are those formed by repeated multiplication. As shown in Case 24, "Folding paper," the relationship between the number of times a piece of paper is folded in half and the number of sections the creasing forms is exponential. With each fold, the number of sections doubles.

The important properties of a relationship in which there is repeated doubling are shown in both the table and graph below.

Number of Folds	Number of Sections
1	2
2	4
3	8
4	16
5	32
6	64
7	128
8	256

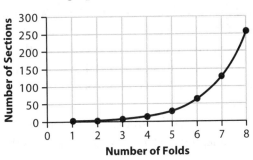

At first glance, one might think there is no significant difference between square relationships and this new kind of relationship. The values in the output column of the table increase rapidly, just as the number of tiles in the Growing Square pattern, and the graph bends upward, as does the graph of the Growing Square pattern. It is true that the graph that results from folding paper bends upward much more sharply than the graph from Growing Squares, but this could be a difference of degree and not a difference of kind.

One way to see the difference in the two relationships is to look at the pattern of *increase* of the numbers in the output column. The Growing Square table shows the result of *adding* 3, then *adding* 5, then *adding* 7, then *adding* 9, and so forth. In the Folding Paper table, the output results from *multiplying* by 2, then *multiplying* by 2, then *multiplying* by 2, and so forth. However, multiplying a number by 2 is the same as adding that number to itself. This says, then, that the amount one *adds* to any given value is equal to the value itself; that is, in the Folding Paper table, the pattern of increase is given by 2 *added to* 2, then 4 *added to* 4, then 8 *added to* 8, and so forth. Thus, the sequence of *changes*—2, 4, 8, 16, ...—is not linear but is exponential.

While repeated multiplication characterizes exponential functions, the number multiplied need not be 2. For example, if the piece of paper is repeatedly folded into thirds, you would still have the exponential function, $y = 3^x$— where x is the number of times you have created thirds, and y is the number of sections. The value of the places in our place-value system is an exponential function—$y = 10^x$— where x is the number of places to the left of the ones place and y is the value of the place. If a savings account earns 5 percent interest each year, and the interest is reinvested, the amount in the account is $y = m(1.05)^x$, where m is the initial investment, x is the number of years the account has been open, and y is the total amount in the account.

When we consider any of these formulas to define a function on the entire number line, the graph no longer resembles that of a quadratic function.

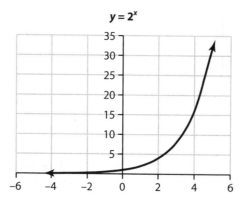

4.3 • Other nonlinear functions *There are many categories of such functions.* In this section, we have explored the best-known and most common nonlinear functions. However, the possibilities for kinds of relationships between pairs of quantities are endless. One can simply invent more and more complicated algebraic expressions and study the patterns of behavior between their variables.

There are also many other important and still relatively simple rela- 715 tionships between quantities that exist in nature. In Session 7, through the Ferris-Wheel problem you came across a *sine* function. One characteristic of the sine function is that it is *periodic*: a basic pattern is repeated infinitely.

Sine Function

Another kind of function is an *indirect proportion*, in which the product of the two variables is constant. From Session 2, the gift-giving context—in which a number of people contribute equally to a \$36 gift and the amount of 720 each person's contribution is a function of the number of contributors—is an example of an indirect proportion. If n is the number of people contributing, $\frac{36}{n}$ is the amount each person contributes. If we consider the function $y = \frac{36}{x}$ on the entire number line except 0, its graph has two disconnected parts. Note that there is no value for $x = 0$ because $\frac{36}{0}$ is undefined. 725

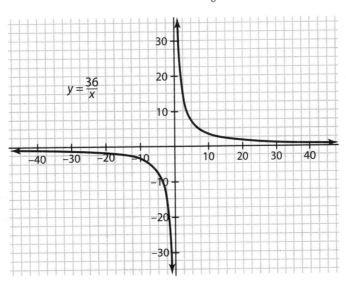

5 • DATA-BASED FUNCTIONS *Functions may be determined by data and be governed by no underlying formula.*

In Chapter 7, Cases 27–29, students collect data on temperature, volume, and height over time, recording their data in tables and graphs. They develop important skills around these two modes of representation so crucial in mathematics and science. Many of the issues touched upon in the previous section—how patterns of change appear in tables and graphs—also arise in these cases. However, the tables and graphs do not express such underlying formula-based relationships between quantities, as do the linear relationship between the number of pennies in a jar and the number of days of collecting pennies or the quadratic relationship between the area of a square and the length of its side. In fact, the data do not express any underlying formula-governed relationship. The data *define* the function.

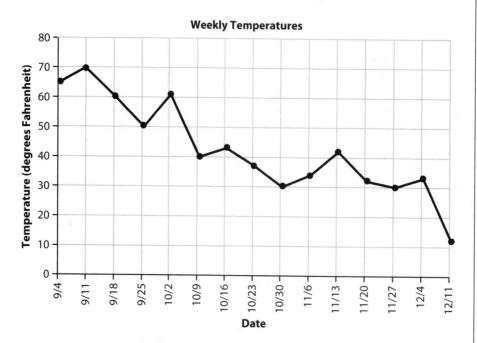

This graph is of the temperature recorded once each week by the students in Case 27, "How low will it go?" The 15 points on the graph define a function that can be studied in much the same way as the basic functions described in the previous sections. Not only can one ask, "What was the temperature on September 25?" one can also ask, "What are the trends?" The data are in agreement with the usual pattern of temperature variation in the Northern Hemisphere, with a general trend downward from

September to December, though from one week to the next, temperatures might rise or fall. However, as the students in the case are learning, we do not take the data as reflecting some deeper law or formula. A meteorologist might try to derive an algebraic expression that "fits" this data in order to analyze patterns or construct models to predict the weather. Whatever her reasons for constructing such an expression, the meteorologist would not do so because she believes that there is an expression that determines this data. Nonetheless, the techniques we use to interpret the data are the same as those we would use if it were given by a rule.

Note that the graph shows the discrete data points based on the information that students obtained. It certainly makes sense to consider temperatures between those points, but the lines drawn on the graph between data points do not necessarily reflect the actual temperature on those days. For example, there may have been a spike in temperature between September 18 and September 25, or the temperature may suddenly have dropped, but this information is not available and so is not seen on the graph.

In Case 28, "Melting snow and ice," the class places loose snow, packed snow, and crushed ice in graduated cylinders and measures the volume of each substance as it melts over a 2-hour period. The graph below displays the students' measurements for the loose snow.

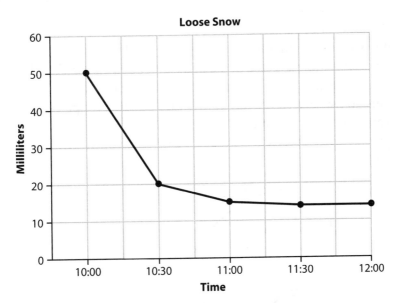

We can see that the volume of the material in the cylinder initially decreases but then levels off. We know this not only by making rough readings from the points on the graph but by observing that the curve of the graph, which is drawn in to help us see relationships, drops and then becomes horizontal. By noticing that the line of the graph is steeper from 10:00 to 10:30 than from 10:30 to 11:00, we can also see that the volume dropped faster in the first 30 minutes than it did during the next 30 minutes. In drawing this conclusion, we use the same kind of analysis that we did with the quadratic functions: The graph appears curved because the *changes* in the dependent variable (outputs) are themselves changing.

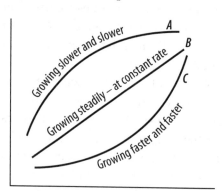

In order to examine the issues around the shape of a graph and a pattern of change, let us briefly consider the highly idealized graphs of the height of three plants. The top graph plots the height of plant *A*, the middle the height of plant *B*, and the bottom the height of plant *C*. The graph of plant *B* is perfectly straight; that suggests growth at a constant rate, which is in contrast to the shape of the graph of plant *C*, which bends upward and suggests faster and faster growth. Likewise, the graph of plant *A* continues to rise, even as it has a downward bending shape, suggesting that plant *A* is growing but at a slower and slower rate.

Similarly, we can study graphs of a situation when the dependent variable is decreasing.

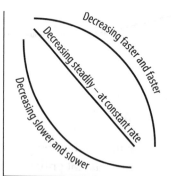

Just as we have seen with graphs of linear, quadratic, and exponential functions, the shape of the graph of data-based relationships affords information not only about a quantity but also about the changes in that quantity.

6 • THE CONCEPT OF FUNCTION *Just as number is a central concept of mathematics study in the elementary grades, function is a central concept of mathematics study in middle and high school—and beyond.*

In this essay, we have explored three families of relationships between quantities: linear functions, including direct proportions, nonlinear functions of several categories, and data-based functions. One might easily conclude that these are entirely separate concepts, with only the most general and ambiguous resemblances among them. Some have rules; others do not. Some graphs are straight lines, others curved. We explore complicated patterns of arithmetic in some and hardly mention arithmetic in others. What they do have in common is that in each situation, there is a set of inputs (an independent variable), a set of outputs (a dependent variable), and a correspondence, of some kind, from each input to one output. This common theme among these situations points to the essential characteristics of what mathematicians call a function.

Just as number is a central concept of mathematics study in the elementary grades, function is a central concept of mathematics study in high school—and beyond. In the same way that younger children build toward an understanding of the abstract concept of number over many years of experience, it makes sense that students should spend many years *before* high school gaining experience with a variety of relationships necessary for an understanding of the concept of function (Davis, 1985; NCTM, 2000; Smith & Thompson, 2007; Yackel, 1997). These students are not only building toward a big idea in mathematics, but they are also learning an important use of the ideas of algebra (Kieran & Chalouh, 1992; Carraher & Schliemann et al., 2001; Carraher, Schliemann, & Schwartz, 2005). Such work is not simply preparation for future courses but is significant mathematics in itself, which extends the problem situations in elementary- and middle-school mathematics and challenges students.

We have explored in this essay a basic set of relationships among quantities. These relationships are basic in the sense of being archetypical: They are the *forms* by which we think about and describe situations of change. The numerical relations between ingredients in a recipe should be of the same kind as the relationship between eyes and noses in a room. If you want to charge for your services, you should charge in proportion to the time you work, except possibly for some fixed costs, such as rent and insurance.

What is intriguing about these basic relationships is not just the way in which values of the output are related to values of the input, but also the way *changes* in the output are related to the *changes* in the input. If you double the sugar in a cake recipe, you should double the flour. If you double the time on a job, you should expect to double your pay, but you cannot expect to be paid for your fixed costs twice. Then there is the pleasant surprise that other, more complicated, relationships also have *change-to-change* patterns of these types. If you build certain kinds of growing patterns of tiles, then the rule that relates the number of tiles necessary to build an arrangement with a certain number of tiles in the base might be very complicated, but the *increase* in the number of tiles required as you increase the size of the base goes up steadily and forms a linear relationship.

Thus the study of functions has led us to a basic idea of the mathematics of change. We have studied relationships in which there are two quantities, an input quantity and an output quantity. But it is not simply a matter of tracking the particular values of input corresponding to particular values of output. Of equal interest is the way in which *changes in input correspond to changes in output*. In so many issues, such as with global warming and population, the problem is not just the current state but also the *rate of change* in the current state. The language of functions allows us to better describe and understand these changes.

References

Billings, E.M.H., & Lakatos, T. (2003). Lisa's lemonade stand: Exploring algebraic ideas. *Mathematics Teaching in the Middle School, 8*(9), 456–460.

Borba, M., & Confrey, J. (1996). A student's construction of transformations of functions in a multiple representational environment. *Educational Studies in Mathematics, 31*, 319–337.

Carraher, D. W., & Schliemann, A. D. (2001). *Can young students operate on unknowns?* Paper presented at the XXV Annual Conference of the International Group for the Psychology of Mathematics Education, Utrecht, The Netherlands.

Carraher, D. W., Schliemann, A. D., & Schwartz, J. L. (2007). Early algebra is not the same as algebra early. In J. Kaput, D. W. Carraher & M. Blanton (Eds.), *Algebra in the early grades* (pp. 235–272). Hillsdale, NJ: Erlbaum.

Confrey, J., & Smith, E. (1995). Splitting, covariation, and their role in the development of exponential functions. *Journal for Research in Mathematics Education, 26.*

Confrey, J., & Smith, E. (1994). Exponential functions, rates of change, and the multiplicative unit. *Educational Studies in Mathematics, 26*(2–3), 135–164.

Confrey, J., & Smith, E. (1991). *A framework for functions: Prototypes, multiple representations, and transformations.* Paper presented at the 13th Annual Meeting of the North American Chapter of the International Group for the Psychology of Mathematics Education, Blacksburg, VA.

Davis, R. B. (1985). ICME-5 report: Algebraic thinking in the early grades. *Journal of Mathematical Behavior, 4*(2), 195–208.

English, L. D., & Warren, E. A. (1998). Introducing the variable through pattern exploration. *The Mathematics Teacher, 91*(2), 166–170.

Healy, L., & Hoyles, C. (1999). Visual and symbolic reasoning in mathematics: Making connections with computers? *Mathematical Thinking and Learning, 1*(1), 59–84.

Kaput, J. J. (1989). Linking representations in the symbol systems of algebra. In S. Wagner & C. Kieran (Eds.), *Research issues in the learning and teaching of algebra* (pp. 167–194). Reston, VA: National Council of Teachers of Mathematics.

Kieran, C., & Chalouh, L. (1992). Prealgebra: The transition from arithmetic to algebra. In D. T. Owens (Ed.), *Research ideas for the classroom: Middle grades mathematics* (pp. 179–198). New York: Macmillan.

MacGregor, M., & Stacey, K. (1993). Seeing a pattern and writing a rule. In I. Hirabayashi, N. Nohda, K. Shigematsu & F. Lin (Eds.), *Proceedings of the 17th Conference of the International Group for the Psychology of Mathematics Education*, Vol. 1, 181–188. Tsukuba, Japan.

Monk, S. (2003). Representation in school mathematics: Learning to graph and graphing to learn. In J. Kilpatrick, G. M. Martin & D. Schifter (Eds.), *A research companion to principles and standards for school mathematics* (pp. 250–262). Reston, VA: National Council of Teachers of Mathematics.

Monk, S., & Nemirovsky, R. (1994). The case of Dan: Student construction of a functional situation through visual attributes. *CBMS Issues in Mathematics Education, 4,* 139–168.

Moschkovich, J., Schoenfeld, A., & Arcavi, A. (1993). Aspects of understanding: On multiple perspectives and representations of linear relations and connections among them. In T. Romberg, E. Fennema & T. Carpenter (Eds.), *Integrating research on the graphical representation of functions* (pp. 69–100). Hillsdale, NJ: Lawrence Erlbaum Associates, Inc.

NCTM. (2000). *Principles and standards for school mathematics.* Reston, VA: National Council of Teachers of Mathematics.

Nemirovsky, R., & Tierney, C. (2001). Children creating ways to represent changing situations: On the development of homogeneous spaces. *Educational Studies in Mathematics, 45*(1–3), 67–102.

Nemirovsky, R., Tierney, C., & Wright, T. (1998). Body motion and graphing. *Cognition and Instruction, 16*(2), 119–172.

Noble, T., Nemirovsky, R., DiMattia, C., & Wright, T. (2002). *On learning to see: How do middle school students learn to make sense of visual representations in mathematics?* Paper presented at the Annual Meeting of the American Educational Research Association, New Orleans, LA.

Noble, T., Nemirovsky, R., Wright, T., & Tierney, C. (2001). Experiencing change: The mathematics of change in multiple environments. *Journal for Research in Mathematics Education, 32*(1), 85–108.

Orton, J. & Orton, A. (1994). Students' perception and use of pattern and generalization. In J. P. daPonte & J. F. Matos (Eds.), *Proceedings of the 18ᵗʰ Conference of the International Group for the Psychology of Mathematics Education*, Vol. 3, 407–414. Lisbon, Portugal.

Piaget, J., Grize, J.-B., Szeminska, A., & Bang, V. (1977). *Epistemology and psychology of functions.* Dordrecht, Netherlands: D. Reidel.

Russell, S. J., Tierney, C., Mokros, J., & Economopoulos, K. (1998). *Investigations in number, data, and space.* Glenview, IL: Scott Foresman.

Smith, E. (2003). Stasis and change: Integrating patterns, functions, and algebra throughout the K–12 curriculum. In J. Kilpatrick, G. M. Martin & D. Schifter (Eds.), *A research companion to principles and standards for school mathematics* (pp. 136–150). Reston, VA: National Council of Teachers of Mathematics.

Smith, J. P., & Thompson, P. W. (2007). Quantitative reasoning and the development of algebraic reasoning. In J. Kaput, D. W. Carraher & M. Blanton (Eds.), *Algebra in the early grades.* Hillsdale, NJ: Erlbaum.

Tierney, C., & Monk, S. (2007). Children's reasoning about change over time. In J. Kaput, D. W. Carraher & M. Blanton (Eds.), *Algebra in the early grades* (pp. 185–200). Hillsdale, NJ: Erlbaum.

Tierney, C., Nemirovsky, R., Noble, T., & Clements, D. (1998). *Patterns of change: Tables and graphs. A unit of investigations in number, data, and space.*

White Plains, NY: Dale Seymour Publications.

Yackel, E. (1997). A foundation for algebraic reasoning in the early grades. *Teaching Children Mathematics, 3*, 276–281.

Zaskis, E., Dubinsky, E., & Dautermann, J. (1996). Coordinating visual and analytic strategies: A study of students' understandings of the group D_4. *Journal for Research in Mathematics Education, 27*(4), 435–457.

940